C000195021

Also by M J Harper

The History of Britain Revealed
(USA title: The Secret History of the English Language)
The Megalithic Empire (with H L Vered)
Meetings with Remarkable Forgeries

DVDs

A New Model of the Solar System
The Distribution of Deserts
The Megalithic Empire

YouTube

The Megalithic Empire
www.youtube.com/watch?v=IJ_S6zkh_PY

Websites

The Applied Epistemology Library
www.applied-epistemology.com

The Megalithic Empire
www.themegalithicempire.com

AN UNRELIABLE
HISTORY OF THE
SECOND WORLD WAR

M J Harper

Urquhart Press
urquhartpress@gmail.com

Lightning Source (UK) Ltd
Chapter House, Pitfield
Kiln Farm, Milton Keynes MK11 3LW

www.lightningsource.com

Published by Urquhart Press 2018

Copyright © M J Harper 2018

The author asserts the moral right to
be identified as the author of this work

A catalogue record for this book is available
from the British Library

ISBN 978-0-9542911-3-6

Typeset in Sitka Heading

All rights reserved. No part of this publication may be
reproduced, stored in a retrieval system, or transmitted, in any
form or by any means, electronic, mechanical, photocopying,
recording or otherwise, without the prior permission of the
publishers.

Contents

1	Britain's *Drang Nach Osten*	1
2	The Great Dictators	3
3	Teschen: Cause of the Second World War	8
4	Up For The Cup	15
5	Maginot Line Vindicated	20
6	The Manstein Plan	22
7	Why the Cheesemonkeys Surrendered	25
8	German Ship Rocks World	29
9	Neutrals for the Asking	34
10	Neutrals for the Taking	38
11	Roosevelt Leads from Behind	40
12	The Lion, the Bear and the Wardroom	44
13	What Hitler Should Have Done	51
14	Balkan Follies	56
15	You Win Some, You Lose Some	59
16	By Any Other Name	61
17	Tanks: the Penny Packet Theory	64
18	Michael Wittman vs The British Empire	74
19	Aces High	77
20	Airmindedness	84
21	The Wooden Walls of England	89
22	Beacon of Light	93
23	Jews in High Places	96
24	The Holocaust: For or Against?	101
25	Napoleon and Hitler	113
26	Gentlemen and Players	121
27	Behind the Wire	130
28	Going Down With The Ship	135
29	Senior Service	137
30	Getting What You Wished For	146
31	How Intelligent Are Armies?	152
32	Airborne Soldiers, Chairborne Generals	157
33	First Rule of Fight Club	167
34	Last Knockings	180
35	Who Won The War?	182
	Index	187

1 Britain's *Drang Nach Osten*

By the summer of 1939 Britain had come to the realisation that war with Germany was inevitable. Using the privilege accorded to island nations, she started casting round for people to fight the war for her. France was already signed up, Italy and Japan were allies of Germany, the USA was an island nation and had chosen to sit this one out. That left Russia.

Fortunately the Russians deployed the world's largest military forces and their national interests were not only at odds with Germany's but the two countries could not be more ideologically at daggers drawn. On the other hand the Russians knew perfectly well they were the only game in town and would be making stiff demands for their alliance. The British who are dab hands in counter-perfidiousness decided, since the Russians also had nowhere else to go, not to show too much enthusiasm and sent off a very low-level delegation. To make sure the Russians got the message it went by sea. In the fast-moving events of 1939 spending a week getting there was a signal nobody could miss.

Stalin was taken aback. He did intend making demands of the British but he was a worried man. He knew war was coming and needed allies in place when it did, so when the British eventually arrived he lost no time getting down to negotiations. "What most concerns me," he began, "is that when it comes to war with Germany, should things get sticky, you British can always go home to your little island, we Russians can't. If you really want me to put my head in a vice you'll have to say how many divisions you can provide to fight alongside the Red Army."

1

The British delegates whispered amongst themselves and finally the Russian interpreter said, "Seventy."

"Seventy?" said Stalin in outraged tones. "You clearly know nothing about fighting on the Eastern front. Seventy divisions won't last three months."

There was another pause and another flurry of whispered conversations among the British delegation and then their interpreter said, "Your interpreter seems to have mis-heard. We said seventeen divisions."

"Seventeen? You're offering me seventeen divisions?"

"No," said a British delegate, "I think there's been some crossed wires. We are planning to have seventeen divisions in active service when war is declared but that has to cover all our needs."

Stalin: "So how many divisions am I going to get?"

British delegate: "Well, we plan to mobilise a field army of five divisions but that's promised to the French for the Western front. Everything else is earmarked for home and empire, what with the Japanese situation and so forth."

Stalin: "So you are saying I'm getting nothing at all?"

British delegate: "The Navy has a marine brigade. We could deploy it to Murmansk if that would help."

At this point a flunky entered the room and whispered in Stalin's ear, "Comrade General Secretary, Herr Ribbentrop is in the antechamber."

*   *   *

2 The Great Dictators

We carry around this notion that the Second World War was all about Democracies versus Dictators. Not so. The two largest armies fighting on the side of the Democracies were those of the dictators Joseph Stalin and Chiang Kai-shek. At least one fully paid-up democracy, Finland, was fighting with the baddies. Nor should we forget that British, French and American colonial troops would not altogether go along with the idea they were fighting for democracy. Nevertheless we assume the war was mostly about taking on the Axis, a natural alliance of dictators, Hitler and Mussolini, the gruesome twosome. Not so. Aside from Mussolini not being particularly gruesome, the two were by no means natural allies. Only blunders by the Democracies drove them together.

Their personal relationship was more equivocal than the newsreels allow. Hitler was, it is true, an admirer of Mussolini—his 1923 Munich Putsch was modelled on the 1922 March on Rome—and he continued to show faith up to and even after Mussolini was overthrown. Mussolini did not always reciprocate, at first because Hitler was 'jumped up', later because he was the reverse. Neither man permitted sentiment or ideology to dictate foreign policy which was just as well because the relationship between Italy and Germany has been subject to sudden reversals.

Ever since the two countries emerged in the middle of the nineteenth century they have been neither natural allies nor natural opponents. They could choose. They chose, for instance, to be allies between 1882 and 1915 whereupon Italy chose to be an opponent. It was the same story after the Great War. Sometimes Italy and Germany were 'fellow victims of Versailles', sometimes Italy remembered she was a 'victor of Versailles' and this on-off pattern continued after the Nazis came to power in 1933.

Hitler was determined that Italy and Germany be allies. The main source of tension between the two countries was the South Tyrol, German-speaking but annexed by Italy in 1919. Its 'return to the Reich' was a touchstone not only for German Nationalists but for all Germans who, like the rest of us, tend to be nationalistic with a small *n*. All Germans except Hitler, who argued that South Tyrol was best left Italian. The assumption that Hitler was a demagogue telling Germans what they wanted to hear is wide of the mark. He was an intellectual of considerable gifts who worked out from first principles what Germany needed, then convinced his fellow Germans they needed it too.

Hitler did believe that *Austria* should be part of the Reich, Mussolini very much thought it should not be. This was straightforward zero-sum advantage: if Germany controlled Austria, Italy would not only have a Great Power on her northern border she would have competition in the Balkans, her own special area of influence. Mussolini stopped the *Anschluss* by making enough noise, militarily and diplomatically, to prevent Germany taking over Austria, giving Hitler a stinging rebuff. This was in 1934 but as it runs counter to the Great Dictators narrative the episode has been lightly airbrushed despite it being a critical moment in the run-up to the Second World War.

At this time the democracies did not know they were 'the democracies', they regarded Italy as simply a fellow member of the Great Power club, vexatious about Mediterranean issues but nothing France and Britain could not handle. When Hitler came to power they did not suppose they were now confronted by 'two dictators', they only knew this new Germany might threaten the status quo, to which they were quite attached since it consisted of France and Britain running the show. This Austrian business suited them nicely because Germany being at loggerheads with Italy over Austria and already at loggerheads with Russia over revolutionary ideology, meant they only had to attend to their own disputes with Italy to isolate Hitler completely. Let him squawk, France and Britain would continue to run the show. Unless they threw it all away.

Which they now proceeded to do with dazzling speed. In 1935 Italy invaded Ethiopia (then known as Abyssinia). Nothing wrong with that—Britain and France have been invading African countries since the seventeenth century and are still doing so in the twenty-first century—but apparently in 1935 the rules were different. The French and the British (as opposed to France and Britain) were incensed by the Italian aggression and demanded 'something must be done'. That's democracies for you. So something *was* done, that's democracies for you. Not enough to save Ethiopia but enough to assuage delicate consciences. That's democracies for you. More than enough though to incense Italians who understandably cried 'hypocrisy!' and were in such a bate Hitler only had to make clucking noises for Italy to walk right in.

When the Spanish Civil War started in 1936, the line-up was Britain and France versus Italy and Germany. *Now* it was democracies versus dictators: Spanish Democratic Government/Britain/France vs Spanish Dictator Franco/ Mussolini/Hitler. Not for long. The most dictatorial regime in human history, Stalin's Russia, came in on the democratic side, figuring that lining up with democracies and supporting legitimate governments would get their own lapses in these areas overlooked, and an invitation back to the top table was sure to follow. They should have known better. France and Britain announced that outside interference in a civil war was anathema and would Russia kindly desist. Italy and Germany did not desist, Franco won and a hostile middling power was established on France's southern border and Britain's Gibraltar frontier. The Russians returned thoughtfully to their own affairs.

Flushed with such an easy success, Italy and Germany went on a roll. Italy finished off Ethiopia and invaded Albania; Germany took over Austria (now with Italy's acquiescence), rectified boundaries at Memel and mopped up Czechoslovakia. Because history likes tales of Guilty Men and Stirring Redemption these events are portrayed as triumphs for wily and wicked Dictators, defeats for stupid and supine Democracies. Not so. Any Great Power can have triumphs expending assets on objectives that other Great Powers do not think worth opposing. It is the price paid down the road that matters.

When the road ran out in September 1939, with the two Dictators busy pursuing their own personal agendas, they had fatally diverged. Mussolini had no interest in Poland, he was appalled by the Nazi-Soviet Pact and he refused to go to war. Germany was completely isolated against the combined strength of France and Britain (and Poland). Just because the democracies would be defeated militarily in 1940 is no reason to deny the Appeasers their *diplomatic* success before the war. That is the purpose of pre-war manoeuvring: solidifying your own side and fracturing the opposition.

There were not many people in France or Britain (or the British Dominions or European neutrals or the USA or the world) who thought a war in 1938 would be a sensible idea. Well done, Neville, you can shake your umbrella at any twenty-twenty hindsighters taking issue with your judgement. That would be everyone.

*   *   *

3 Teschen: Cause of the Second World War

In 1919 France was determined to prevent another war.
The best way of doing this, she thought, was to be at the
centre of a system of Great Powers supportive of this noble
ambition. As a nice corollary, for the first time since the
Napoleons, oncle et neveu, France would be the Arbiter of
Europe. There were excellent auspices for their 'Versailles
System':

1. Woodrow Wilson's America made a perfect guarantor
   but would not otherwise interfere
2. Britain had a large army poised to fight but only
   when summoned by France
3. Weimar Germany was to be the new Sick Man of
   Europe, holding on to France for fear of something
   worse
4. Italy would be a nuisance but at most a Mediterranean and Balkan nuisance
5. Russia, which France always finds difficult to control,
   would be excluded by a cordon sanitaire.

No sooner was the ink dry on the Versailles treaty than
perfidious Albion ('Zut alors, there are two of them now')
stepped in. Or in America's case, stepped out. They had
had enough of European entanglements, let them sort out
their own problems. The British, who had learned long ago
that being the World's Policeman is not as profitable as
being the World's Shopkeeper, demobbed Kitchener's
army and resumed her ancient vigil as the guarantor of
European peace (English-style).

With America out, Britain half out, Russia and Italy to be
kept out and Habsburgs and Ottomans just *out*, where was

help against Germany to come from? Could this new League of Nations act, as the Papacy once had, as a Power in its own right? Definitely not, decided the French, the League could only act as the Arbiter Power and that position was already taken. It would though make a fine cat's paw for France as Arbiter Power.

The language of diplomacy is not French by accident. It has not ceased to be French by accident. They cooked up an ingenious scheme: if the cordon sanitaire was capable of keeping Russia out, might it not be equally suited to hemming Germany in? Poland and Czechoslovakia together would be strong enough to cause Germany concern but not strong enough to cause France concern, and the proposal for a 'Little Entente' consisting of France, Poland and Czechoslovakia (with the benevolent support of Britain) was launched. But would it fly? Would these brand new, still struggling nations want to take part in the expensive and dangerous business of Great Power politics?

You bet they would. Poland had once been the largest country in Europe, Bohemia had once been its fulcrum, both wanted nothing better than to strut the stage once more. What's the point otherwise? Parfait! But could they be relied on to be solidly anti-German? That was a given. Each had been carved out of German territory, each possessed large German minorities, each was chronically nervous about German revanchism. But what could these tenderfoots bring to the French table? In combination, quite a lot.

The Poles account themselves a martial race and had just proved it by defeating the Red Army and annexing half the Ukraine. The Czechs were not so keen on fighting, their national hero is the *Good Soldier Schweik*, but they did have a world-class arms industry—in the next war the Germans conquered France using Czech tanks, the standard British Bren gun stood for Brno-Enfield. One last box needed ticking, could they act together? Not clear. Consciousness of a glorious past meant Poland and Czechoslovakia held an exalted opinion of their real importance in the world, and while this is natural enough—we British are born with the condition—they felt an irresistible urge to talk down to one another, making face-to-face negotiations awkward.

The first item on the agenda was the County of Teschen. Teschen had previously been part of the Bohemian province of the Austro-Hungarian Empire (awarded to Czechoslovakia) but more naturally formed part of Galicia (given to Poland). The Poles began negotiations in their preferred style, sending in troops and announcing Teschen's annexation. The Czechs reacted in their preferred style, asking the French to demand the Poles withdraw and start talking. Poles talk as well as they fight and explained they were simply acting in accordance with this new principle of self-determination. Teschen was majority Polish and they had the last Habsburg census to prove it. The Czechs, who talk better than they fight, pointed out these 'Poles' didn't even speak Polish. It's 'Old Polish', retorted the Poles.

This continued without a settlement in sight until it was suggested Teschen might profitably be partitioned. After all, said the French patiently:

1. the south was where most of the Czechs lived
2. the north was where most of the Poles lived
3. the south had a railway vital to the Czechs because it was the only link between two parts of Czecho-

slovakia (and useless to the Poles for the same
reason)
4. the north had the capital city, agreeable to Polish
pan-nationalism (the Czech/Slovaks were not so
keen on pan-nationalism)
5. the south had the coal, abundant in Poland but
lacking in Czechoslovakia
6. the north had the industry, abundant in Czechoslovakia but lacking in Poland

So partitioned it was and both sides got satisfaction.
Nothing upsets people like knowing the other side got
satisfaction. The Poles, reflecting they could have had the
whole of Teschen were it not for those meddling French,
chose only to see brothers and sisters groaning under a
foreign lash. They nursed a grievance against Czechoslovakia (and France) in a way only Poles can. The Czechs,
a much less neurotic nation, made a note that forming
alliances with people who wish to dismember one might
not be such a good idea after all. The Little Entente was
stillborn and the Europe of Four Powers (plus the League
of Nations) made its hesitant way through the Jazz Age.

Not to worry. As long as France maintained control, as
long as Germany was prepared to be controlled, Britain
could be complacent, Italy could chafe and Russia could
pursue socialism in one country. Everything changed
when Hitler came to power in 1933. Not only for Britain
and France but for Poland and Czechoslovakia; though
not, in the absence of the Little Entente, for Poland *and*
Czechoslovakia.

If Country A has a large area coveted by Country B, it
may be better for A to make friends with B rather than

11

forming alliances against B. Or so thought the Poles (A) who proceeded to:

1. ally themselves with B (Germany) in 1934
2. were vindicated in 1938 when B dismembered Cz at the Munich Conference and
3. told A she could help herself to Teschen until
4. a few months later B helped herself to A.

How would events have played out if the Little Entente had become a reality, if Poland and Czechoslovakia had decided to be good neighbours, willing partners with one another and with France? Presumably most things would have remained the same

1. Hitler comes to power in 1933
2. Britain unilaterally destroys the Versailles System with the Anglo-German Naval Agreement of 1935 to protect her own position
3. Germany (the Sick Man), having been given the amber light by Britain (the Guarantor Power) is now free to displace France (the Arbiter Power) if it can
4. Hitler thinks it can and remilitarises the Rhineland in 1936 to see whether it sticks
5. Lacking British support, France can do nothing
6. If France cannot control Germany, she is no longer the Arbiter Power
7. Germany tests whether she is the new Arbiter Power by invading Austria
8. None of the Powers contest this
9. Germany is the new Arbiter Power
10. But facing a combined Poland and Czechoslovakia.

If the French (and the British) were unwilling or unable to control Germany there was nothing Poles and Czechs, either separately or together, could do about it. But if there had been a united front of Poles *and* Czechs, the Munich

Conference would have gone quite differently. There could not have been a Munich Conference at all in the sense of a peaceful settlement of German claims on Czechoslovakia underwritten by the other Powers. If the Little Entente had been a reality one of those Powers would have been Czechoslovakia/Poland and they would certainly not have underwritten such an outcome. Poland had German minorities of its own to worry about and showed the following year it was quite prepared to fight in order to keep them. Czechoslovakia could hardly do less when it was her own German minorities at stake, being allied to Poland and France and maybe Britain.

Now if the other factors at the time were still in play— the chief of which was British and French reluctance to fight a world war over whether Germans might be allowed to live in Germany—there would probably not have been a war in 1938, but that 'probably' is critical. Assuming everything else is still the same there is no doubt the Wehrmacht would have beaten Poles-and-Czechs in 1938 as easily as they beat Poland alone in 1939 but that was *not* the issue in September 1938.

Germany was by then unarguably the dominant power in Europe but Hitler was not unarguably the dominant power in Germany. He still had the Wehrmacht to contend with and it is very unlikely he would have put his dominance to the test by asking the army to take on Czechoslovakia *and* Poland (for certain), France (probably), Britain (possibly) and Russia (just possibly). We cannot say whether there would have been a war and who would have joined in but that is the point: Hitler could not say either. He could not assure the Wehrmacht who they would be fighting, and he most definitely could not predict what their answer would be. That is the difference between open-ended wars and

13

peace conferences fixed in advance. One thing Hitler did know in 1938 was that if the answer from the generals came back 'no', there would likely be no more Hitler, so he would not have asked in the first place.

Or maybe he would! He was like that. Maybe the Wehrmacht would have said 'yes'. They were like that. Maybe a war starting in 1938 would have had a different outcome. Wars are like that.

*   *   *

14

4   Up For The Cup

If you have the misfortune to support a lowly football club
there is a consolatory game you can play. Early in the
season your team, Grimsbottom Rovers, beat some bunch
of wallies but that same bunch of wallies later on happen
to draw with Manchester United in an obscure cup competition. That means Grimsbottom are better than Man U.
Stands to reason. The form guide says so: A beat B, B drew
with C, A beats C.

Not even you actually believes this because no matter
how much you love t'Grims and no matter how much we
all hate Manchester United, it cannot be ignored they are
in the Champions League and Grimsbottom are mid-table,
UniPants Division Three. The form guide is trumped by
results week in, week out. One-off upsets are always possible but in football everyone knows their place and everything else is wishful thinking. Wars are not fought every
week, there are no league tables, there is *only* the form
guide: who beat who last time out.

Great Powers can, broadly speaking, decide whether to
fight wars and that decision will be predicated on three
factors

1. Winning a war can be advantageous
2. Losing a war is always disastrous
3. Predicting the outcome of a war is inherently difficult

which creates a paradox. If going to war is a voluntary act
how can two Great Powers, looking at the same set of
facts, go to war? How can both think they will win, and
with plenty to spare given the uncertaties? There must

be some wishful thinking going on so let us sort out the Grimsbottoms from the Manchester Uniteds of the Second World War because, it seems, some of the Great Powers could not work it out for themselves.

The war started in July 1937 when Japan invaded China. Although Great Powers are supposed to be able to choose whether to fight wars there is some doubt—even now—whether 'Japan' decided on war with China. It was an unfortunate incident triggered by junior officers acting off their own bat, or so the story goes. Even so it was *Japan* that decided to convert a minor skirmish into a full-fledged war. China of course did not choose to go to war with Japan but her government, insofar as China had a government, could have sued for peace at any time. This had always been her policy: put up a show of resistance, then buy off the barbarians with concessions. More milch cow than Great Power.

The Japanese were acting strictly according to the form guide. In 1894 they had defeated China quickly and profitably. In 1931 Japan (or a cabal of Japanese army officers etc etc) had provoked an incident on the Japanese-controlled Manchurian railway which had necessitated an invasion of Manchuria, war with China, token resistance by China, Manchuria being handed over by China. In 1937 something had changed. China did not sue for peace, did not buy off Japan, she just kept on fighting. Not well, not successfully, not perhaps wisely, but she did. She was becoming a Great Power.

This latest war was of little use for updating the other Powers' form guides. Everyone beats China. 'Everyone except us apparently,' mused the Japanese, for whom the full-time whistle seemed an eternity in coming. Could they meanwhile arrange a fixture against someone just as beatable as China but more inclined to recognise when they were beaten? In 1938 and again in 1939 the Japanese provoked small wars with Russia. Form was once again on their side as they had comfortably and profitably beaten the Russians in 1904, but now there was a complete reversal. The Russians defeated the Japanese, and rather easily at that. Again the other Powers took little interest, border skirmishes being strictly pre-season friendlies, but the Japanese could not avoid noticing the Soviet Union seemed a more formidable opponent than Tsarist Russia. They quickly wrapped up the war, signed a non-aggression pact and started looking round for easier matches.

The Russians for their part had also taken note but did not entirely concur with this idea that the Soviet Union was stronger than Tsarist Russia. While the latter did have a distinctly patchy set of results, their own record consisted solely of *Poland 1 USSR 0*. Still, with the east now quiescent might they chance their arm in the west against some carefully selected opponent? What about Finland, a country so new, so minor league, it had no record at all? No record means no form guide and the Finns fought them to a surprise pyrrhic draw.

Hitler too was looking at the form guide, always kept meticulously up to date in Germany because of the number of contiguous Powers she may have to go up against. Her strength is such that she can be confident of defeating any other single Power which is to be expected—Germany could not exist as a Great Power were it otherwise—but the contiguous Powers know it too and try to avoid single combat with her. Thus Germany's constant game plan is to isolate opponents and fight short wars lest other Powers join in. The 1939 German form guide read

17

1. The French were nearly beaten in 1914 with half the German army
2. Russia was beaten in 1917 with half the German army
3. The whole German army was beaten in 1918 by a combination of Britain, France and the USA.

Hitler adopted a strategy to address the situation. The Molotov-Ribbentrop Pact removed Russia for long enough to ensure an undivided German army would beat France before either the British or the Americans could effectually intervene, then he occupied France to keep the Anglo-Americans out long enough for a mano a mano with Russia.

Germany's occupation of France in 1940 was of intense interest to the Far Eastern Powers—French Indo-China now being available virtually free of charge. The British hastily made concessions to the Japanese to ensure they went for French territory rather than their own. The unwisdom of appeasing dictators, Churchill decided, only applied in Europe. Japan occupied Indo-China without a war.

The Americans had Far Eastern possessions too but, with no German complications, they started making aggressive countermoves against Japan. Isolationism, they decided, only applied in Europe. This obliged the Japanese to dig out their USA form guide. There wasn't one! The Americans had never fought a Great Power war apart from taking on some distracted Brits in 1812 and manning a bit of the front line against Germany in 1918. Otherwise it was all banditos and hidalgos and people with bows and arrows. Some of those they lost. The Americans, the Japanese decided, were well worth a punt.

Not so fast, Nippon, always read the notes at the back of the book. The USA happens to be one of only three Great

Powers in recorded history—alongside the Roman Republic and the Mongols—that have had not just the strongest army in the world (there must always be one of those) but the *two* strongest armies in the world. In 1863 the USA had put the Federals and the Confederates into the field. Japanese familiarity with world history did not go back further than the Meiji Restoration of 1868.

The Second World War broke out because nobody had spotted the significance of that 1939 result, *Soviet Union 1 Japan 0*. This was no border incident, no giant-killing one-off pre-season cup upset, it was a straightforward case of one Great Power, Japan, choosing not to go to war with another Great Power, Russia. The Powers were also forgetting the advice of that doyen of conflict resolution, R. F. B. Shankly, 'Form is temporary, class is permanent'. Russia had been a Great Power since Poltava in 1709 and while Russian results over the centuries *were* mixed, 'mixed' means the form guide itself is unreliable. Germany paid no heed and came unstuck in the Great Patriotic War.

The USA in its turn ignored the small print: 'Late kick-offs not included in some editions.' Their form guide did not carry the *China 0 Japan 0* result and they got a bloody nose taking on the Chinese in 1950. At which point the form guides could be closed forever because nuclear weapons have consigned Great Power wars to history. Unless it's early doors.

*   *   *

5 Maginot Line Vindicated

Ever since German unification in 1871 French foreign policy has been driven by two overriding concerns: Germany is stronger than France and Germany is right next door. France's standard solution is to make sure Russia is onside and Germany's strength divided, a strategy that has worked well enough right up until General de Gaulle and the Fifth Republic.

But not always. In 1917 Russia was forced out of the First World War and Germany could at last concentrate against France. By then Plan B was in place—line up other anti-German Great Powers alongside—and France, Britain and the USA together prevailed in 1918. Both solutions lapsed immediately after the Great War when the Russians retired behind a cordon sanitaire (of French making!), the British gave up on large armies and the Americans gave up period. What was to be Plan C?

Build the Maginot Line. This was not, as historians opine, an expression of French feebleness. That is an expression of historians' feebleness because the Maginot Line had a number of eminently practical functions:

1. it was carefully sited to force Germany to invade via Belgium
2. which would bring in Britain
3. not to mention Belgium
4. as well as being a 'force multiplier'.

Fixed defences like the Maginot Line, though costly, allow small forces to hold long sections of the front. So, put elderly reservists to do a holding job along the Maginot Line, station the main field army on the Belgian frontier and establish parity with the Germans long enough for the British to get their act together. When the balloon went up in 1940 the Maginot Line worked exactly to specification. The British and Belgians were in place and the Allies had achieved, not parity, but a comfortable superiority. What went wrong?

Not the Maginot Line which remained largely un-breached until captured from the rear. It was something else entirely, something neither the Maginot's designers nor anyone else could possibly have planned for. Nations in the west—the French, the British, the Belgians and later the Americans—had lost the ability to slug it out on the ground with those in the east still prepared to do so—the Germans, the Russians, the Japanese and the Chinese. In the Second World War, whenever west was matched against east, it was futile relying on a 'comfortable superiority'.

However, the Second World War introduced another novelty: material abundance might produce military diffidence but it also produces material abundance. It was discovered that Western matériel could prevail against Easterners slugging it out on the ground if there was time to convert the margin from a 'comfortable superiority' into an 'overwhelming superiority'. The British were given that time thanks to the English Channel, the Americans were given that time thanks to two oceans. The French only had the Maginot Line.

*   *   *

6   The Manstein Plan

One of the most cited rationales for the Anglo-French defeat in 1940 is the Manstein Plan. Originally the German General Staff had put forward a very orthodox strategy, attacking through Belgium, essentially repeating the campaign of August 1914. Generals always start off fighting the last war, a wholly sensible policy, so the Anglo-French high command had predicted this and placed most of their troops on the Belgian border. To make sure all were reading from the same page, a German courier plane carrying the battle plans landed on the wrong side of the border so the Belgians, the French and the British were able to prepare for the coming German onslaught at their leisure.

There matters stood until Erich von Manstein, an obscure but ambitious general fretting on the moribund eastern front, decided his best chance to get into the action would be to offer up a plan of his own to Hitler. This proposed going through the Ardennes rather than through Belgium. The Belgian attack would still go ahead but now *as a feint* using infantry, to fix the main Allied armies, while the armoured divisions would strike much further south, through a weakly held part of the line, then swing round behind the French, reach the Channel coast, thereby cutting off all the enemy forces still engaged in Belgium.

Hitler liked the idea for two reasons: firstly, the Allies knowing the current plan made him understandably nervous and secondly, he was always on the lookout for ways to épater his generals. The Manstein Plan was handed over to the General Staff to run the numbers, do the war gaming and sum up the prospects. It was a non-starter, they said, the Ardennes road network was so poor traffic jams would quickly build up, indeed they would extend all the way back over the Rhine. Only spearheads would ever make it to the Meuse in time to prevent the French redeploying from the north. The French were sure to have good defences in this sector because it was precisely where the Germans had beaten them not in the last war, but the one before that, the Franco-Prussian War of 1870.

Hitler adopted Manstein's plan anyway and the attack proceeded exactly as the General Staff had warned. Despite being unopposed in the forward zones (the French had correctly concluded this was no place for a modern army), the German motorised and panzer units quickly became snarled up in the twisty, hilly lanes of the Ardennes. Traffic jams really did stretch back across the Rhine. Still, this being the German army, progress of a sort was maintained and soon the leading echelons were debouching into the Meuse Valley to take on the prepared French defences.

It is true the Manstein Plan achieved complete tactical surprise but there was no obvious reason for the French to be concerned. As the German General Staff had foreseen, only a few panzer units were able to make contact and the French could bring up their reserves and switch their northern forces more rapidly using the excellent French communication net than the Germans could bring up their own troops through the Ardennes. That was not the problem. The problem facing the French was to decide whether this actually was the main German attack because up in the north the 'feint' was sweeping all before it! The lumbering old horse-drawn German infantry in Belgium were having just as much success as the thrusting armoured divisions in the south. What on earth was going on?

The famous Schlieffen Plan, a surprise German attack through neutral Belgium, had failed by a narrow margin in 1914 when the quite unprepared Belgians held the whole advance up long enough for the French to re-orientate their defences and halt the Germans in front of Paris. Second time round, this did not happen. Despite knowing they were in the firing line, despite having built hugely expensive fortifications, despite having had eight months to prepare, the Belgians were brushed aside. Forts meant to hold up an advance for weeks were captured in *hours*. Belgian, French and British armies meant to hold up the Germans for years lasted *days*. The Wehrmacht poured through on all fronts and against all opposition. The Manstein units in the Ardennes made the most spectacular progress, being motorised that was inevitable, but the infantry divisions in Belgium were doing every bit as well, just slower.

The campaign was wrapped up in short order when the Belgians surrendered, the British skedaddled and the French sued for peace. Why are we not told this? Why is it all 'blitzkrieg' and 'unorthodox axes of advance'? Nobody likes being told their soldiers did not put up much of a fight so they are told it was down to the Manstein Plan. Not, for some reason, the Hitler Plan.

*   *   *

7 Why The Cheesemonkeys Surrendered

History, they say, is written by the victors so heroes tend to come from the winning side. But there is always room for a gallant loser like Paul Reynaud, the French Churchill (hooray!) who became Premier in March 1940, taking over from Edouard Daladier, France's Neville Chamberlain (boo). The story that Reynaud was dominated by his mistress, a closet fascist, is a canard put about by his opponents and will not be dignified by repetition here.

The main decision facing Reynaud on taking office was what to do about the head of the French army, Général Gamelin. The relationship between governments and generals was a delicate one in the Third Republic (and in the First, Second, Fourth and Fifth Republics) so Reynaud could not immediately dismiss Gamelin even though he suspected his commander-in-chief was out of touch with modern trends. The fact that Gamelin would not permit a radio at his field headquarters lends some credence to this but anyway the general was still en poste when the German offensive began in May. Its rapid success gave Reynaud a number of options

1. He could leave Gamelin in place on the grounds that no matter how feeble your horse, changing it in mid-torrent may not be advisable
2. He could sack Gamelin and replace him with one of the subordinate commanders, say Huntziger or Giraud, who were fully appraised of the situation
3. He could skip a generation and appoint a younger corps commander, Altmayer perhaps or Aymes, who were at the sharp end

4. He could think outside the box and decide, as this seemed to be a new kind of war, to appoint a junior tank specialist like de Gaulle

5. He could think outside the box in the other direction and appoint Marshall Petain, France's First War defensive supremo, who would provide an unchallengeable rallying point for French forces

6. He could appoint the 73-year-old Weygand who had no knowledge of either modern warfare or the immediate situation because he had been packed off to deepest Syria, where he still was, and would take an absolute age even getting back to France, never mind taking up the reins of his new command.

Reynaud the Fox pounced. Gamelin was sacked, Weygand summoned and France surrendered.

Historians are in a quandary about exactly why. As it was the Germans who had surrendered to the French in 1918 something must have changed in between. When historians are in a quandary they do not say 'We are in a quandary', they start hurling reasons at their audience in such profusion that quandary is the last word that springs to anybody's mind. Here are twenty reasons they give for Why France Fell:

1. The French were commanded this time by a dunder-head called Gamelin

2. The French armed forces had been fatally infected by the defensive Maginot Mentality of right-wing governments in the twenties

3. The French armed forces had been fatally infected by the pacifism of left-wing governments in the thirties

4. The French birth rate was declining (the German birth rate not as much)

5. The flower of French youth had died in the 14-18 trenches (the flower of German youth had been re-placed)

26

6. Refugees clogged up the roads for the French army (but not the German army)
7. The Belgians surrendered prematurely without telling the Allies
8. The British withdrew prematurely without telling the French
9. The Germans used the Manstein Plan, the Allies were expecting the Schlieffen Plan
10. The Germans employed the brilliant Blitzkrieg technique
11. The French had too few planes especially modern ones
12. The British had lots of planes especially modern ones but refused to send them to France
13. French infantry were still using 75 mm guns from the First War
14. French tanks were dispersed, the German ones concentrated
15. German tanks had radios, French ones didn't
16. German tanks used petrol so could refuel at French garages
17. French tank commanders in their undermanned cupolas had too many tasks to undertake
18. The British did not pinch out the panzer thrust from the north because of the half-heartedness of the French to the south
19. The French did not pinch out the panzer thrust from the south because of the half-heartedness of the British to the north
20. La Belle France was lost because …. [fill in present day societal failing that most gets writer's goat].

The real reason is simple but boring. The last time Germany advanced into France, during the Spring offensive of 1918, they made rapid gains and reached Amiens before being turned back by a combination of a very large French army, a very large British army and a very large American army. In the Spring offensive of 1940 the Germans made rapid gains, got beyond Amiens and reached the Channel coast, severing the French army in two and defeating it in detail. The difference this time? No great British army, no great American army, no great mystery.

*　　　*　　　*

8 German Ship Rocks World

In December 1939 a German naval squadron was prowling the South Atlantic with a commerce-raiding brief. It consisted of the *Graf Spee*, a so-called 'pocket battleship', and the *Altmark*, a freighter acting as supply ship. One of these was destined to play a pivotal role in global grand strategy for the rest of the war, but which one? To answer this question, we need to know What Happened Next.

The *Graf Spee* had on board a number of British merchant navy officers rescued from ships she had sunk (Captain Langsdorff was a Good German) and these were transferred to the *Altmark* which was dispatched to make her own way back to the Fatherland. Langsdorff then plotted a course for the estuary of the River Plate where he knew there would be merchant ships taking Argentinian beef to Britain.

Commodore Harwood RN with a squadron of three British cruisers had anticipated this, resulting in the famous Battle of the River Plate. Langsdorff, though the very model of a modern major commerce raider, was an indifferent naval commander. Instead of standing off, using his 11-inch guns on the British 6-inch and 8-inch cruisers and then speeding off as pocket battleships were designed to do, he decided to fight it out. After sustaining some superficial damage the *Graf Spee* retreated into Montevideo harbour and requested, as was its right under international law, forty-eight hours to make repairs.

This triggered a worldwide media storm since a German fox cornered in a neutral lair with British hounds waiting for him to come out made great copy. Langsdorff did come

29

out eventually but sportingly scuttled the *Graf Spee* in the Plate Estuary thus avoiding the loss of any further lives on either side. Except his own—he shot himself in a Buenos Aires hotel room in the best traditions of the Kriegsmarine.

All this had tremendous ramifications. The British got a sorely needed morale boost, neutral opinion throughout the Americas was greatly impressed and Adolf Hitler, disgusted by *Graf Spee*'s pusillanimous performance, scrapped plans for building major surface units for the German Navy, thus determining its role for the rest of the war. So yes, you guessed correctly, it was the *Altmark* that was destined to affect the entire Grand Strategy of the Second World War.

By some miracle, or perhaps incompetence, but definitely not British intent, the *Altmark* evaded the Allied blockade and reached northern Norway in February 1940, where her captain faced a dilemma. There was little chance of evading British patrols in the North Sea so he entered Norwegian territorial waters to make his way to Germany through 'the Leads', the islands and fjords of western Norway. Technically, as soon as he entered neutral Norwegian waters he would have to allow his British prisoners their freedom, and he had no intention of doing that.

To understand the labyrinthine events that followed it has to be borne firmly in mind that the only actual fighting going on anywhere in Europe was between Russia and Finland. Not, one would think, of central importance to the British and the French fighting the Germans, but this is to ignore another fact: the British and the French thought they were winning the war. 'The Germans have made no effort on the Western Front,' crowed the French, 'and everything is in place if they do. It'll be 1914 all over again.'

'It's one thing stopping the Germans,' said the British, 'but they only surrendered in 1918 when the blockade starved them into domestic insurrection.' 'Good point,' everyone agreed, 'and there's no chance of that while they can get what they need from the Russians.' The solution? Make war on Russia of course. Or at any rate send troops to help the Finns on such a scale Stalin would think twice about cosying up with Hitler. The only impediment to the plan (aside from taking on the world's two foremost military powers simultaneously) was that to help the Finns, the Anglo-French forces would have to cross neutral Norway and Sweden. Neither Norwegians nor Swedes agreed to this, not wishing to take on the world's two foremost military powers simultaneously.

Never deterred from a bad idea, the British came up with a new scheme. The *Altmark* was not the only German ship making use of the Leads, Swedish iron ore was reaching Germany that way while the Baltic was frozen. 'Why don't we mine the Leads, thereby forcing the German iron ore ships out of neutral waters and into the North Sea where we can capture them?' 'Won't the Norwegians get a bit upset about having their neutrality violated?' 'Of course they will and the Germans will rush to their support giving us just the pretext we need to get into Norway. Sweden will accept force majeure and we'll be in Finland.' What could go wrong?

What went wrong was the Finns making peace with the Russians in time to save the Anglo-French from their folly but meanwhile the *Altmark* was creeping down the Leads. The Norwegians were perfectly aware they were at the centre of Great Power intrigue and had to act, as do all neutrals caught up in a war, with extreme circumspection. To appease the British they boarded the *Altmark* on three separate occasions to 'search for contraband'; to appease the Germans they managed on each occasion to miss several hundred British seamen banging and hollering below decks.

Churchill, First Lord of the Admiralty, knew what was needed and sent destroyers into Norwegian waters to flush out the *Altmark* and rescue the sailors. He was just about entitled to do this on the grounds that the Norwegians were not properly protecting their neutrality and in London, Paris and neutral capitals (other than Oslo) this was hailed a triumph of neo-Nelsonian Diplomacy. In the German capital somebody was watching the Altmark incident with much keener eyes.

Hitler had been greatly alarmed by the Russo-Finnish war. He *thought* he had nullified the Soviet Union with the Molotov-Ribbentrop Pact, assuming that Russia would only have signed with its bitterest enemy out of pure funk. This was true but funk or no funk Russia cannot help but be Russia and Stalin used the breathing space provided by the Pact to expand in all directions. He occupied the Baltic states, adjoining Germany's iron ore routes from Sweden; attacked Finland, the key to Germany's Scandinavian flank; began pressurising Romania to cede Bessarabia, next door to Germany's oil supplies in Ploesti, and repositioned the Red Army along the new Russo-German border in Poland. Far from having a quiet and co-operative Russia in the east, it seemed to Hitler he had let loose a raging bull.

This is the point at which the *Altmark* entered Grand Strategy. Hitler knew Britain would not have breached Norwegian neutrality over a few seamen, the reason must be that Britain wanted to make Norway some kind of de facto protectorate for a further push into Scandinavia. But why? Britain had no obvious strategic interests there. It could only mean that Britain and Russia were somehow in league, which would explain Stalin's brazen behaviour. If Britain and France were to join with Russia, the line-up so disastrous for Germany in the Great War would be in place once again. Any such connection must be nipped in the bud. This was all completely illusory though Hitler, who prided himself on both his intuition and his mastery of grand strategy, was half right because Britain did indeed invade Norway on the 9th of April 1940, to lay mines in the Leads, a policy that failed when the Germans arrived the following day and forced them out.

Although the Norwegian campaign was a remarkable success in itself, it was fatal for Germany in the long run because it encouraged Hitler to continue making dramatic forays to places equally off the military map, in Yugoslavia, Greece, Crete, Libya, Tunisia, Sicily and Italy. When the crux of the war arrived, during the Russian campaign, Germany found herself chronically short of troops. There were twelve divisions doing nothing very much in Norway itself but vastly more carrying out highly avoidable duties everywhere from the Dodecanese to Anzio.

It cannot be said the *Altmark* decided the outcome of the Second World War but in such a finely balanced contest it might have.

*   *   *

9 Neutrals For The Asking

Two countries at opposite ends of the Mediterranean played vital roles in the war by *not* participating in it. Spain and Turkey made no bones about which side they preferred—Germany and Britain respectively—but both would be profound disappointments to their Great Power patrons.

The Axis had been instrumental in bringing Franco to power in 1936 (literally, the Germans flew him and 2,500 of his troops from Morocco at the start of the Spanish Civil War) so they felt entitled to be paid back in kind. All Franco had to do was invade Gibraltar, or allow the Axis to invade Gibraltar on his behalf, and the debt would be met in full. And why wouldn't he? Like all Spaniards, Franco passionately wanted Gibraltar back and in October 1940, when he and Hitler parleyed in a Pyrenean resort, there was only one winner of the Second World War. But the Spanish dictator told the German dictator to shove it. I put it like that because it is how Hitler experienced the rebuff, Franco being the one person *in the world* able to have this effect on the Führer. Quite why demands an explanation.

In the First World War a procession of neutrals—Turkey, Italy, Romania, Bulgaria, Greece—had actually clamoured to join in because a) they knew which side would win and b) the winners would reward them. Half of them guessed wrong and the other half discovered that Great Powers do not necessarily reward small powers once their usefulness is at an end. They *all* discovered their soldiers were killed in staggering numbers and their homelands trampled over by uncaring armies. Win or lose, those forgoing neutrality during the war did not prosper after it. As that last great neutral, Woodrow Wilson, was also to discover. Franco stayed out for the six years of the Second War and stayed in power for thirty years after it.

Not wholly out of it. Neutrality is never enough, it has to be creative neutrality. At the outset Spain's neutrality was one-eyed but only in a minor sort of way: refuelling U-boats in Vigo, reporting Allied naval movements through the Straits, low level stuff. Pro-Axis enthusiasm was held in check by the British murmuring they didn't *have* to let Spanish wheat imports through the blockade. Events took a more serious turn in 1941 when Franco sent troops to fight against Russia but he was able to scramble back to a less partisan position in 1942 by studiously not interfering with the Anglo-American landings in North Africa, something that had been taxing the minds of Allied planners. This meant, after the war, and in the face of bitter Russian protests, the Anglo-Americans allowed the last fascist regime in Europe to continue. They even cocked a snook at the Russians by getting Franco to join NATO. He gave up the neutrality but not the fascism.

Franco is a lesson to all neutrals. Ignore your own ideological leanings, never try to predict winners, bob and weave as if your life depended on it because it often does. But he also provides a lesson for Great Powers: friendly neutrals can be a real nuisance. A neutral but pro-Axis Spain was an *Allied* asset throughout the war because Hitler could hardly invade Spain to grab Gibraltar, overthrowing a dictator he had just helped to install. Franco ended up protecting Gibraltar from the Germans at no cost to the British.

Turkey's position was almost a mirror image. Despite being pro-British, the best way the Turks helped was by doing everything possible *for the Germans*. When the Axis occupied the Balkans in 1941 they presented a pincer threat to the British in the Middle East. With Rommel's Italian-German armies in Libya threatening Egypt from the west, only Turkey stood in the way of an advance from the north. Hitler could have invaded Turkey, as he could have invaded Spain, but again he hesitated. Was a benevolent Turkey more valuable to him than an occupied Turkey?

The Turks did all in their power to persuade him it was by increasing supplies of strategic minerals to Germany, by permitting free passage for Axis ships through the Straits, by denying the same privilege to the Allies and by refusing to countenance Allied military forces anywhere on or near her territory. Even the British soldiers training the Turkish army in the arts of modern war had to wear mufti. Never mind where her sympathies lay, Turkey knew where her dangers lay. Turkey feared a German victory but not half as much as she feared a Russian one and in June 1941 Britain and Russia were on the same side.

All things considered, the Turks concluded, it was better to stay out of this one though they omitted to mention this to the British who were supplying them with generous amounts of scarce war supplies in the belief that eventually Turkey would have enough weaponry to make it safe to enter the war, a point never quite reached. Churchill kept urging Turkey to join the war, kept sending equipment, kept training the Turkish armed forces, kept forgetting the British weren't really all that important. Needless to say, after the war, the Turkish governing party stayed in power even longer than Franco.

In wartime Great Powers tend to assume, 'If you're not with us, you're against us.' They often go one step further:

'If you're not with us, you're downright wicked.' Remember the Swedes? The Irish? How dare they look after their own national interests. Don't they know there's a war on?

* * *

10   Neutrals For The Taking

The 'rape of Belgium' in 1914 branded Germany indelibly as a ruthless invader of neutral countries that got in her way. The Second World War soon showed the Hun had not changed its spots but this is not entirely fair, or at least it is not entirely balanced. That traditional cherisher of small nations, Great Britain, was at it too.

In fact the British started it by invading neutral Norway in April 1940 to mine its territorial waters. The Germans were not far behind, arriving the day after. Indeed they were already ahead two-to-one in the Rape of Neutrals because they had occupied Denmark en route. The British themselves were not averse to serial Scandinavian invasions and started piling troops into the Norwegian port of Narvik with its easy access to some very valuable iron ore fields they had spent months deliberating whether to occupy or not. That would be the *Swedish* iron ore fields.

It never came to pass because the Narvik troops were needed elsewhere. The Germans had surged further into the lead in May 1940 by invading three neutrals—Belgium, Holland and Luxembourg. The British were determined to keep up and in September they attacked neutral French West Africa, but retreated after a whiff of Vichy grapeshot. The Race for Neutrals was put on hold for the winter but in April 1941 the Germans started it up again by invading Yugoslavia. The British performed a brilliant tit-for-tat by occupying Iraq in May, then showed Jerry a clean pair of heels by invading Syria and Lebanon in June, Iran in August and Madagascar in May 1942.

The Americans were novices in the Neutrality Stakes and needed their hands held by the British when they invaded Morocco, Algeria and Tunisia in November 1942. The following year the two scallywags popped the Portuguese Azores into the pot. That more or less wrapped it up for the Second World War but shortly thereafter these same peace-loving democracies set up the United Nations which solemnly declared that invading neutral countries was outlawed henceforth and forever.

Since when the pair, in unison or separately, have invaded the following neutral countries, depending on one's interpretation of 'invasion', 'neutral' and 'country'

Afghanistan	Guyana	Pakistan
Albania	Haiti	Panama
Angola	Honduras	Paraguay
Bolivia	Iceland	Peru
Brazil	Indonesia	Philippines
Cambodia	Iran	Puerto Rico
Chile	Iraq	Sierra Leone
China	Italy	Somalia
Colombia	Laos	Sudan
Cuba	Lebanon	Syria
Dominican R	Liberia	Uruguay
Egypt	Libya	Venezuela
El Salvador	Nicaragua	Yemen
Greece	North Korea	Yugoslavia
Grenada	North Vietnam	Zaire
Guatemala		

11 Roosevelt Leads From Behind

The American presidents generally held in highest esteem are Washington, Lincoln and the two Roosevelts. All are coincidentally associated with triumphant wars: the Revolutionary War, the Civil War, the Spanish War and the Second World War respectively. The likelihood of great presidents only being around when great wars are around is not statistically great, but then again American presidents find it difficult to make their mark at home, what with states' rights and laissez-faire, so the best way into the pantheon is by doing something dramatic abroad. But be warned, you cannot cheat by starting a war, you just have to be there when it is brought to a triumphant conclusion.

Historians (and Americans, and the world) judge by association rather than analysis, a shortcoming illustrated by historians' (and Americans' and the world's) judgement on Franklin Delano Roosevelt. He is a giant for *two* reasons: curing the Great Depression *and* winning the war. We need not dwell on the depression lasting longer in America than anywhere else, President Roosevelt was certainly there when it was brought to a triumphant conclusion. We are concerned here solely with the Second World War.

Leading up to which FDR is unanimously credited with being on the side of the angels. He tried, you will recall, to do everything he could to oppose those awful right-wing dictators but his hands were constantly being tied by those awful right-wing isolationists in Congress. Or, putting it another way, the most powerful man in the world sat on his hands while the world went to hell in a steady procession of hand-carts.

Things changed in 1939. Now there was a great demand for armaments so American industry could polish off the slump by providing them. The armaments would go exclusively to the side of the angels which was easily achieved because the British were blockading everybody else. In 1940 things changed again when France fell and German submarine bases were established along the Atlantic coast, triggering the Monroe Doctrine. Never mind Roosevelt, all presidents have to obey the Monroe Doctrine: that outside powers must not be allowed to threaten the Americas. It was high time for the USA to become the Arsenal of Democracy.

What did the British require most to protect those ships filled to the gunnels with American supplies? Well, said Churchill, what we really need is more escort ships. I'm glad you asked, said Roosevelt, because we've got fifty mothballed destroyers left over from World War One which weren't much cop then, are obsolescent now and will take an age to get into any kind of shape for taking on modern U-boats. We'll take 'em, said Churchill. Not so fast, said Roosevelt, you'll have to pay for them. We can't, said Churchill, we've got no money. Fair enough, said FDR, we'll take naval and air bases in Newfoundland instead. You've got a deal, said Churchill. And the Bahamas, Jamaica, St Lucia, Trinidad, Antigua and British Guiana. You've got a deal, said Churchill.

In 1941 things changed again. Japan bombing Pearl Harbour, Roosevelt agreed, meant war with Japan but he was silent about Germany and Italy. Germany and Italy declaring war on him tipped the scales. The British sighed with relief. With the Americans now comrades-in-arms their own problems were over and they sent a high-level delegation over to Washington for discussions about joint strategy, combined production programmes, all the things comrades in arms talk about at the onset of a war. They found nobody to talk to. The Americans seemed nonplussed at the very notion of war planning. In their system the president is supposed to do that and Roosevelt had, what with one thing and another, not done any. Never mind, the Americans would operate a kind of bran-tub system. Whoever needed anything put their hands in and took whatever they could grasp. The British speedily discovered there were bigger hands than theirs in Washington but it didn't matter. It was the biggest bran tub in history.

Roosevelt showed his true worth in his wartime foreign policy. Nowadays we are used to the CIA and the NSA running their own foreign (and domestic) policies but neither of these existed in 1941, they were both borrowed off the shelf from the British. The problem under Roosevelt was that the State Department, the Treasury, the Navy, the Army and the Senate all had *their* own foreign policies and not only did Roosevelt fail to prevent them pulling in different directions, he would often add an extra wheel by capriciously taking over any area that took his fancy without reference to anyone else. He decided, for instance, that China was to be his own special preserve and not just because the fragrant Madame Chiang Kai-shek was always hanging around the White House. He also conducted a personal correspondence with Churchill, laying down grand strategy (or having it laid down to him) to the exasperation of his professional advisers. To stir the pot he would from time to time dispatch his bagman, Harry Hopkins, around the world to conduct diplomacy on the hoof.

None of this was of much account during the war itself because the bran tub and the Russians were winning it but it did matter when it came to configuring the post-war world. Roosevelt's hero and mentor, Woodrow Wilson, had made a complete pig's ear of this and FDR was determined not to make the same mistake. Away with all that Versailles-style conferencing, he and Stalin would put the world to rights man to man, two old pro's together. One old pro as it turned out but Roosevelt died just in time for President Truman to start putting Stalin back in the box. From then on it just was a matter of finding someone who could put America back in the box.

*   *   *

12   The Lion, the Bear and the Wardroom

Iran was the only country during the war to accommodate British, Russian and American troops making it a perfect test bed for how well these disparate allies could co-operate in wartime, and whether that co-operation would survive the end of hostilities.

Before the war Iran was theoretically an independent country but because the British were running the oil industry in the south and 'helping out' elsewhere, it was recognised by the world, though only grudgingly by the Iranians, that Iran was 'in the British sphere of influence'. Iran was important to the British not just for its oil but for its strategic location

1. adjacent to Iraq, where oil was also important but which was constantly in revolt at being in the British sphere of influence
2. adjacent to India, the jewel in the crown, also constantly revolting
3. adjacent to Russia, Britain's traditional rival in south Asia
4. adjacent to the Indian Ocean and the warm water ports Russia would find so useful for (3).

Britain had been playing this Great Game, as it was popularly called, for centuries and was pottering along quite amiably in Iran until 1941 when a greater game impinged:

1. Germany attacked Russia.
2. Britain was now allied to Russia.
3. Russia badly needed war supplies but
4. Germany sat athwart the sea routes.

5. The best land routes ran through Iran which presented difficulties because

6. Iranian transport infrastructure was not up to the task and since

7. the Iranians were pro-German

8. they were not going to do anything about it.

The difficulties were addressed by Britain invading Iran from the south and Russia invading from the north. The British were very experienced in dealing with Iran and packed the over-complaining Shah off to South Africa, replacing him on the Peacock Throne with his young and terribly grateful (and extremely nasty) son. Content to leave domestic politics to him, the British set about beefing up the railway in the south, from the Persian Gulf up to Tehran, which they already ran because that was where the oil was. The railways in the north, between Tehran and the Russian border, could be left to the Soviets to beef up.

The Russians were not very experienced in Iran but very experienced in the Great Game so they set about competing with the British rather than beefing up the railway. This may seem odd with the Germans hammering on the gates of Moscow, but the Bear is like the scorpion that stung the frog carrying it across the river. It is in its nature. Stalin began Operation Iran by encouraging Azerbaijani separatists in northern Iran to rise up and demand union with their kith and kin in the Azerbaijan Soviet Socialist Republic. Or, as the rest of us would describe it, a large slice of Iran would be annexed by Russia.

Armed insurrection and smoothly running railways do not mix but in any case it soon occurred to Stalin that, properly played, the whole of Iran might fall into his lap. He set up the *Tudeh*, notionally the Iranian Communist Party, which quickly busied itself fomenting insurrection against the central government in Tehran. There being a shortage of Iranian communists, Russian communists had to go into Tehran to get things moving. This raised British eyebrows but, as the Russians explained, the railway to Russia started from Tehran so it made logistical sense to send their own people in. As this was exactly what the British were doing, they lowered their eyebrows. Lacking a friendly shah, the Russians had to resort to buying up Tehran newspapers (everything in Iran was for sale) and soon banner headlines appeared: 'Iranian government a nest of fascists', 'Widespread demands for cabinet reconstruction', 'Tudeh tipped for Interior Ministry', 'Today's train cancellations, see pages 3-8'.

At this juncture a new participant entered the scene. The USA was now in the war (on the British and Russian side) and viewed the Iranian impasse with some bemusement. Clearly the situation called for a swift dose of American can-do. President Roosevelt had an a priori assumption that progressive Russia was better than imperialist Britain, so he sent troops and engineers to can-do the *British* section. The Americans made themselves thoroughly unpopular with everybody and did little for the railways but at least all the relevant players in the Iranian theatre were now present and correct.

Decent supply lines were eventually established and substantial quantities of Anglo-American goods were soon flowing northwards to Russia. Nothing was coming back from the Russians to help their allies but then again it never did. 'Please, Uncle Joe, can we have a few T-34's?' 'No, Uncle Sam, but keep sending us *your* tanks which are completely useless but we can strip out the radios.' This is unfair, the Russians loved their Packard trucks. Besides, two commodities *were* coming back on the railway. Firstly, it was one of the conduits by which Poles not liquidated by the NKVD for being prematurely anti-German were permitted to rejoin the fight alongside the British. Secondly, it brought the food on which mainly desert-bound Iran relied. Or not as the case may be. It depended whether the Iranian government was doing what the Russians wanted and since it often wasn't, the trains came back empty and great numbers of Iranians perished.

Such frog-and-scorpion tactics meant the Iranians, hitherto solidly anti-British, were now solidly anti-Russian. This has no bearing on the political fortunes of countries playing host to the Red Army but it does have a bearing on countries playing host to the Red Army *and* British *and* American armies. With the end of the war in sight, the diplomats in the Foreign Office and the State Department came up with a plan. The best way to get the Russians out, they argued, was for the British and Americans to announce their intention to leave Iran, kit and caboodle, thus putting maximum pressure on the Russians to leave as well. They might not do so but at least they would have to pay the price at the bar of world opinion. That's the way diplomats tend to think.

There was however a diplomatic snag. The Russians had a treaty with the Iranian government permitting them to stay for six months after the end of hostilities. When precisely would that be? At Yalta in February 1945 Stalin had agreed to enter the war against Japan six months after the defeat of Germany, so Russian forces could stay on in Iran for six months after the defeat of Germany; then they could stay on for the duration of the war against Japan; then they could stay on for six months after the defeat of Japan. If they couldn't sovietise Iran in that time they

47

might as well hang up their hammers and sickles. Bar of world opinion? Don't be daft, it would be completely legal.

The diplomats cutely short-circuited this ploy by announcing British and American troops would start leaving immediately. For logistic reasons, the railways for instance were under joint control, 'immediately' would have to be in lock-step with the Russians. 'Very ingenious,' said the British army who would be doing most of the leaving, 'but what does *in lockstep* actually mean?' 'Ah,' said the diplomats, 'that's the cunning part. If we start by evacuating central Iran, where there's no oil, the Russians will have to start leaving central Iran too and that means Tehran. Clever or what?' 'Certainly not clever,' responded the War Office, 'we have summer camps in the central highlands and it will soon be summer.' This genteel tiff between civilians and soldiers continued through the first half of 1945 and the fate of Iran and world geopolitics was put on hold while brass hats defended their right to play upcountry snooker. Finally, Foreign Secretary Eden demanded Churchill order the Chiefs of Staff to fall into line and they did as soon as their next defensive position was prepared.

By mid-1945 Germany was defeated but the war with Japan continued so when the Foreign Office suggested that British forces should now start leaving *southern* Iran, thus pressurising the Russians to evacuate the north, the Chiefs of Staff protested once more. 'How can we leave our oil unprotected at the very moment we need it for our ships on their way to fight the Japanese?' 'But surely,' pointed out the diplomats wearily, 'with the U-boats gone and all the new tankerage built, we are awash with oil.' 'You can never be too careful,' said the soldiers. 'In any case,' said the diplomats, 'we have been pumping oil out of Iran for decades without needing the military to be involved.' 'You can never be too careful,' said the soldiers. These inter-departmental wranglings were particularly unhelpful with the Potsdam Conference looming, but in due course the British and American forces did leave Iran and sometime later, what with the Americans having the Bomb, the Russians left too.

At last the status quo ante could be restored and the British resumed control of Iran with the young Shah as fig leaf. Naturally his first act was to declare the Soviet fig leaf, the Tudeh Party, illegal. Banning parties built for conspiracy is rarely a sound policy and the communists, in alliance with Iranian nationalists, took power in 1951.

To everyone's delight the first act of the new government was to nationalise the oil industry, necessitating the re-naming of the Anglo-Persian Oil Company to British Petrol-eum. Also, and no less pregnantly, Ayatollah Khomeini made his debut on the world stage when he, ahem, came out in support of the Shah, the British and the Americans. We were all young once. The Anglos sighed and after a few phone calls nobody would buy nationalised Iranian oil and government finances plunged into chaos. A few more phone calls put rioters onto the streets of Tehran, the gov-ernment was chased out of town and the Shah was back in power for the next twenty-five years.

Iranians, like a good many people, prefer not having their country run by Anglo-Americans so the Shah could only stay in power by using the SAVAK, a secret police force of the utmost savagery. And ubiquity—it was calculated that a third of the adult male population ended up working in some fashion or other for the SAVAK, edging out their nearest rivals, the East German STASI, who were man-aging with one in four.

The Russians were not going to accept this indefinitely. In 1979 the Tudeh Party and the nationalists decided to have another crack. This time, in the hope of establishing a more permanent regime change, they would add the Islamists. The ayatollahs dealt permanently with the communists and the nationalists and Iran had finally achieved what it had always wanted—true independence from the Great Powers. That is what true independence means, you get what you asked for.

*   *   *

13 What Hitler Should Have Done

In June 1940, after the defeat of France, Hitler had the perfect opportunity to 'do the right thing'. If Britain would not make peace with Germany, Germany would make peace with Britain! In international relations it does not always take two to tango. Being a wallflower can be good strategy too.

This does not come naturally to Great Powers for whom meddling is a way of life but there is a current example of the potential benefits of such a policy. The USA should make unilateral peace with Kim Jong-un, even grant North Korea most-favoured-nation status. They would be surprised how little he could do with no-one to fight. He might invade the south though his family have taken care not to do so for sixty-some years and besides that is the situation now. He might develop nuclear weapons and a delivery system to go with it, except he has already done that. He might rattle around doing all kinds of mischief but, honestly, his scope is strictly limited, or at least as limited as it is now, unless you insist on constantly giving him fresh opportunities to ruffle your hair. You can always take away his most-favoured-nation status. Oh, and by the way, please stop asking China to help out because her chief rival for world dominion finds itself in a complete pickle over North Korea and only China can extricate her. Well, you can ask.

Attack is not always the best means of defence. Defence is not always the best means of defence. Getting others to defend you can be the best means of defence. Following the Armistice with France in 1940 Hitler should have done what the Anglo-Americans would do after the Liberation of France in 1944 and restore France to Great Power status as quickly as possible. Neither the British nor the Americans had any illusions about guaranteed long-term French support but, as Great Power system players, they understood that France stood between them and Germany, between them and Russia, so better a strong France than a weak one.

Hitler was not a system player and did not appreciate that France lay between him and the Anglo-Americans. Nobody, Hitler included, could guarantee what a strong independent France would have done post-1940 but one imperative for all Great Powers is to defend themselves. That surely means against me, supposed Hitler. No, Adolf, that means whoever comes calling and it won't be you, you just left. It might though be the British and the Americans who spent the rest of the war using French territory with relative impunity to attack you. Wouldn't it have been better, as a bare minimum, if they had had to fight the French in order to fight you?

Actually the British *did* have to fight the French at Mers-el-Kébir, at Dakar, in Syria and Lebanon, in Madagascar, in Algeria and Tunisia, but French resistance was always feeble because Hitler would not allow France to punch her weight as a fully restored Great Power. And France would have punched the British good and hard. It suits the world (especially the French) to pretend that Vichy was some kind of aberration born out of fear of Germany but this is as ridiculous as supposing French post-war policies were born out of fear of the Allies. Everyone is impressed by winning sides, everyone conducts foreign policy that suits their situation. France was pro-British and anti-German 1939-40, pro-German and anti-British 1940-44, pro-British and anti-German 1944-57, pro-German and anti-British after Suez had laid the true situation bare.

Having withdrawn his troops and allowed the French complete freedom to choose a foreign policy that suited them, Hitler might have discovered that France would be, as indeed she was, anti-British and pro-German. But that is not all. A defeated but revivified and fully independent France, while presenting no military threat to Germany, would present a military threat to *Italy*. Allies have to be kept in line too. With no France to hold her in check after 1940, Italy embarked on a whole series of Mediterranean adventures that dragged Germany into places that made no sense except for the necessity to support Italy! The gleeful British, who could beat Italians but not Germans, suddenly had a reason to stay in the war. *Another* reason of course.

Hitler should also have withdrawn all German troops from Belgium, Holland, Luxembourg, Norway and Denmark, invited their governments-in-exile to return, even helped to pay for them to get back on their feet. Exactly as those canny Anglo-Americans did after 1945 and which those not very canny Russians neglected to do with their allotment of liberated nations. Would these neutral governments, returning from their imposed exile in Britain, have been anti-German? Of course they would, they'd just been brutally invaded by the swine. So what? What does Germany have to worry about from truly independent and none-too-friendly Belgium, Holland, Luxembourg, Norway and Denmark? Germany's *opponents* would have lots to worry about.

Consider Britain's policy of strategic bombing. Unless the British were prepared to declare war on independent France, Belgium, Holland or Denmark by overflying them,

53

their planes would have to get through the narrow jaws of the Heligoland Bight in order to bomb Germany, a prospect to make even the black heart of Air Marshal Harris quail. Would these pro-British, anti-German countries have permitted British overflying? Would these countries welcome another brutal invasion from those German swine?

A complete German withdrawal in 1940 would have hampered their own military campaigns against Britain—and was presumably why Hitler did not countenance it—but this is typical Great Power thinking. Meddling for meddling's sake. The only thing that should have concerned Hitler in the west was what he could do to the British (and maybe the Americans) vis à vis what they could do to him. His own strategic bombing of Britain would have been restricted for the same Heligoland reasons and his submarines would have suffered from a lack of French and Norwegian bases but, however large these long drawn-out campaigns loom in British memories, they did not loom large in the outcome of the war.

Hitler should have gone further and announced an end to all hostilities against Britain. No submarines in the Atlantic, no Luftwaffe over British skies, no Rommel threatening Egypt. Nothing. Not perhaps the equivalent of granting most-favoured-nation status but what exactly can a bulldog do when there is no-one to bare its fangs at? The British would be free to continue their blockade but experience showed this did little significant damage to Germany, though it would have done a lot to the other countries of western Europe, now at peace and now in a position to make their displeasure felt.

Still, this is the *British* bulldog so let us assume they decide to spend years and years building up their armies on a scale needed to take on Germany. To give them a dog's chance, let us further assume they persuade the Americans to do likewise even though with all quiet on the Atlantic front (except for the British making a nuisance of themselves) they have no obvious reason for doing so. How exactly do our *two* bulldogs get to grips with the Germans? We can ask the Combined Planning Staffs to rank their preferences:

1. Take on some Normandy fixed defences manned by Ukrainians, watched by a disarmed France, then take on the German army
2. Take on defences manned by Frenchmen, then take on an armed France, then take on the German army
3. Bypass an armed France, invade a friendly neutral (take your pick from Belgium, Holland and Denmark), then take on the German army
4. Bypass the neutrals and mount an amphibious assault on Hamburg through the Heligoland Bight.

This last could work if the Germans are away in Russia. It did work, at Inchon in 1950, against the North Koreans. Which is where we came in.

*   *   *

14 Balkan Follies

There are certain places in the world where you ought not to send your armed forces. One is Afghanistan, which did not feature majorly in the Second World War; another is the Balkans, which did.

In 1939 Italy invaded little old Albania. This was successful. In 1940 Italy invaded little old Greece from little old Albania. This was unsuccessful. The Greeks halted the Italians without much fuss and started pushing them back across Albania. The British, who were also at war with Italy, offered to help but surprisingly the Greeks demurred, pointing out

1. they were managing quite well on their own
2. if the British got involved so would the Germans who would not be so manageable
3. but they wouldn't mind a few freebie planes and any other bits and pieces that might be going spare.

Beware Greeks accepting gifts, thought Hitler, who viewed any kind of British presence in the Balkans as a threat to his oil supplies—Romanian wells were in range of Greek-based bombers. So Germany joined the fray against the Greeks which in turn pulled in the British who stopped ejecting the Italians from Libya and shifted their best troops over to Greece in order to re-enact the Battle of Thermopylae. The Germans riposted by re-enacting the Battle of Cannae in Greece and then Libya.

Having been ejected from the Peloponnese the British strongly garrisoned Crete and, with total control of the seas all around, were set fair for the next phase of the war.

The Germans could only come by air which meant not many soldiers carrying not much equipment, but to make it competitive they tipped off the British, via compromised codes, exactly when and where they would be landing. The British were soon back in Egypt set fair for the next phase of the war.

To get to Greece the Germans had elected to go through Yugoslavia. There was no need for this, the original plan had been to go via friendly territory in Romania and Bulgaria, but a palace coup in Belgrade had brought on a Hitlerian fit of pique and he decided to take out Yugoslavia as it were *en passant*. The Yugoslav armed forces were crushed by the usual dazzling all-arms display but the Yugoslav people decided to fight on. Not necessarily against the Germans. The Croats joined the Germans in order to fight the Serbs—if rounding up and butchering hundreds of thousands of Serbs counts as fighting—while the Serbs themselves split into those who wanted to fight the Germans and those who wanted to fight the Serbs who were fighting the Germans.

The same broad picture emerged in Greece as well. It was a maelstrom. Instead of a nice quiet Balkans sending Germany everything she needed, Hitler found he had to pour in German troops just to maintain a modicum of Axis control (the Italians and the Bulgarians were more brutal but less efficient). The British had no need to waste their own troops keeping the cauldron bubbling because the Yugoslavs, like the Greeks, could do it on their own.

Once the Germans were gone, in 1944, the British did start pouring in troops because the people who had been fighting the Germans were communists (bad people) and the people who had been co-operating with the Germans were royalists (good people) and the British are always in favour of good people. They call it 'a moral foreign policy'. Since British regulars were not guaranteed to beat Balkan irregulars, Churchill met with Stalin and wrote some figures on the back of an envelope (apparently literally). Stalin nodded and Greece went to the free world, Yugoslavia went to the communist world. Not for long. Tito broke with Stalin in 1948 and became a member of the free world.

It was a parallel story out east where the Americans were backing the Vietnamese fighting the Japanese (they were called 'the Vietminh') rather than those who had been accommodating the Japanese (they were called 'the French'). But the resistants turned out to be communists so the Americans switched sides. Once Uncle Ho had got rid of Uncle Sam, Vietnamese communism could get rid of Cambodian communism and fight Chinese communism to a standstill. More dominoes like this, please.

*   *   *

15 You Win Some, You Lose Some

1. Name Hitler's most successful battle
2. Name Hitler's most disastrous battle

The answer to question one is the *Battle of Kiev* in which the Germans captured 665,000 Russians. It says a lot about perceptions and realities of the Second World War that the Red Army lost more soldiers in this obscure battle than the total worldwide frontline strength of the British Army at its wartime maximum. But anyway it was the Germans' single biggest success of the war.

The answer to question two is the *Battle of Kiev*. The Russians showed such extraordinary resilience and capacity for improvement that the one chance the Germans had of defeating them was in 1941-2, before the resilience and the improvement had time to kick in. History cannot be rerun but it would appear that defeating the Russians early enough required, as a minimum, the securing of both Leningrad and Moscow in 1941. Taking out these cities would have respectively

1. freed up large numbers of Army Group North
2. joined German forces up with the Finns
3. cut the Russians off from the Baltic
4. eliminated the second most important centre of Soviet armament manufacturing
5. occupied the symbolically important original Capital of the Revolution.
6. occupied the current Capital of the Revolution
7. removed the administrative heart of the heavily centralised Soviet system
8. eliminated Russia's most important industrial area
9. and its chief transport hub.

59

Why didn't the Germans capture these key Russian cit-
adels in 1941? We cannot say they would have but the
main reason they could not have was that in August 1941
Hitler stopped the great panzer drives north and east towards Leningrad and Moscow and diverted the tanks
southwards towards Kiev. He justified this on the not
unreasonable grounds that capturing Russian soldiers in
encirclement battles was better than simply pushing them
back, something he certainly achieved at Kiev.

The German General Staff were aghast at this sudden
change of direction. It was against All Known Precepts of
War. The brilliance of the German General Staff is consistently overestimated—my mum would have been Moltke
and Ludendorff rolled into one with the Wehrmacht under
her command—but in this case they probably knew
whereof they spoke.

*   *   *

16 By Any Other Name

The Second World War was a tank war par excellence and enormous amounts of expertise and planning went into their every detail. Except tank names which were a mishmash.

The word 'tank' itself is a misnomer, thought up by the British in 1915 to disguise their manufacture and employment as mobile water tanks for replenishing the trenches. "Thirsty work fighting the Boche, what?" "Yes, I'll call up some tanks." In the British way, the term stuck. The defining feature, steel caterpillar tracks, was taken from farm tractors though tractors promptly went over to large rubber tyres. I have never understood this.

In France, where the Académie Française outranks the Ecole Spéciale Militaire, the tank is called the *char de bataille*. No wonder they took so long calling them up in 1940. Actually in practice they say *le tank* because secretly the French adore all things British. Not *la tanque*, by the way, should you be thinking of dropping it into dinner party conversations.

Never mix up a tank with the very similar-looking self-propelled gun, an artillery piece mounted on a turretless tank chassis. The Allies should have mixed them up because their tanks were consistently outgunned by German tanks and, since a larger gun can be mounted on a turretless tank, mixing in a few self-propelled guns in their tank units would have solved many of their problems. This was not possible because self-propelled guns count as artillery and the artillery have separate messing arrangements from those ghastly nouveau armoured types. German

61

tanks were consistently outgunned by Russian tanks but, as egalitarians, the Germans soon had more self-propelled guns in their tank units than tanks.

The Germans were also more flexible when it came to naming their tanks. Sometimes they used strident names like Tiger, Panther and Lion but liked to demonstrate their celebrated sense of humour with Elephant, Mouse and Rat. The Elephant was designed by Ferdinand Porsche who should have stuck to volkswagens and sports cars because he left out machine guns and Russian soldiers were soon climbing on board to pop in a hand grenade.

Yet Germany had begun the war with Prussian efficiency—Panzer I, Panzer II, Panzer III, Panzer IV—so was the change in nomenclature policy significant? Possibly. Allied troops in Normandy were prone to 'Tiger Terror', misidentifying all German tanks as Tigers and retreating accordingly. If the Tiger had been known by its technical title of Mark VI, would they have suffered quite so much from Mark VI Terror? Possibly.

The British developed in the opposite direction, starting with whimsy and ending in order. Their best tank of the early years was called the Matilda though not on account of her waltzing ability, having a top speed of eight miles an hour. Their worst tank was called the Churchill which serves them both right. The Cruiser was so called because it was a cruiser tank, lighter but faster than the battleship Matilda. It broke down so often it could not keep up with the Matilda.

The British did take one lesson from the Cruiser, all their tanks would henceforth begin with a C. After the Churchill came the Crusader, the Cavalier, the Centaur, the Cromwell and finally the Comet. We are currently offering the Challenger II to anybody who wants one. Only Oman so far but the first twenty years of a tank's life are always a tough sell. The Challenger did have one good USP: revolutionary 'Chobham' composite armour, which was so effective the concept went worldwide. Invented in Chobham, Surrey, presumably because it begins with a C. Modern sliced white bread was invented in Chorleywood and that too conquered the world, something for post-Brexit Britain to think about.

The best British tank of the war was the Firefly, an American Sherman with a British seventeen-pounder gun. Not a well chosen name because it didn't start with a C and didn't have an insect's bite when up against German tanks, unlike the Sherman. The Americans themselves had the fine tradition of naming their tanks after Civil War generals—the Lee, the Grant, the Stuart and so forth—which was all very well except sending a photo of your Sherman back to the folks in Atlanta, Georgia might be thought insensitive.

The Russians, who built the most effective tanks, lived in a society where everyone was equal but some were more equal than others. They went in for sternly functional names like T-34, KV-1, the Joseph Stalin and so forth.

Did any of this matter? I don't know. What I do know is that there were no high-level committees in any of the warring nations saying, "The tank is the most important weapon of this war, are we going to name them, number them or what?" The point being that, when the *Third* World War starts, and if we have time, there will be focus groups discussing just these sorts of questions. We poke fun at this modern tendency but as Churchill said, Jaw-Jaw is better than War-War.

*   *   *

17 Tanks: the Penny Packet Theory

Tanks were first used, by the British, on a small scale in 1916. They were not a success. Some said this was down to teething problems with the tanks, others said the tanks needed to be used *en masse* concentrated at a single point to make a real breakthrough. There was merit in both arguments and the following year at the Battle of Cambrai more reliable tanks were used *en masse* and with great success. Church bells rang out for the first time in three years. The chimes were still ringing when the Germans rallied and the British were back on their start line.

Nonetheless, by WW1 standards, this was accounted a victory and it was agreed that concentrated tanks used *en masse* was the way to go and this has remained orthodox military doctrine in all armies from that day to this. Proposals to the contrary invariably draw the withering accusation of wanting to use tanks in 'penny packets'.

Tanks and how to use them did not proceed very far in the interwar period partly because nobody could afford to build many tanks in those straitened years, mostly because armies are notoriously resistant to radical upheavals. Theorists in Britain, Germany and Russia did argue for specialised armoured divisions which could advance non-stop without the need for slow-moving infantry and artillery, and got a respectful hearing. It was tried out in manoeuvres and exercises, even small wars if one was available, but how far theory got translated into practice depended largely on the kind of government being answered to. Revolutionary states determined to show New is Best were more receptive than ancien régimes.

The Germans (it is often forgotten that Weimar was a revolutionary regime) and the Russians (though Stalin became less and less revolutionary) experimented with veritable tank armies organised for rapid and independent movement. In fact they experimented *together* deep in the steppes beyond the prying eyes of Versailles inspectors. Rapid movement was obtained for sure but only in one direction, forward. Revolutionary governments are aware any other direction, even planning for any other direction, might spell their doom. This forward-only policy was to have fascinating results when German and Russian tank armies met for real later on.

The British and the French thought in terms of World War One but speeded up. They readily conceded tanks were best organised into brigades and divisions (i.e. not penny packets) but they were to be used as adjuncts to the infantry (i.e. in penny packets). When the tanks did finally roll into action in 1940, the world was agog to find out who was right. It turned out to be the British and the French, though it took a while for anyone to discover this.

We have not quite discovered it yet. If we look at those modern panzermeisters, the Israeli Army, we see that tanks *en masse* storming across deserts win wars. The Americans took their cue from this and stormed across the desert in Desert Storm I and Desert Storm II. Both Israelis and Americans were only following in the tracks of the original desert tank maestros, the British, who stormed across the north African desert against the Italians in 1940. The German panzerkorps underlined the lesson by storming back across the same desert against the British in 1941-2. Tanks *en masse* get the job done as long as the Egyptians, the Iraqis, the Italians and the British are rubbish. If the opposition is halfway decent it is the tanks that are rubbish. Literally. Burning hulks litter the battlefield as the tanks are picked off the moment they break cover crossing the start line. You just can't miss 'em.

In the early days of the war there was a scarcity of half-decent opponents. The Germans overwhelmed the Poles and then overwhelmed the French and the British. Massed tanks, it seemed, were marvellous when overwhelming people so everybody concluded it was the tanks that were doing the overwhelming. This was true in the limited sense that tanks could dislocate the enemy rear, capture his command centres and shatter his will to resist but *getting there* was another matter.

Tanks were only doing the job that cavalry had been doing for thousands of years, exploiting a battle already going the right way and turning it into something more decisive. For those thousands of years competent armies had understood how cavalry were to be used

1. You stuck your cavalry on the flanks.
2. You *could* open a battle with a cavalry charge because
3. if you scattered their cavalry then you might gain a decisive victory but
4. only if your cavalry didn't disappear for the rest of the day chasing their cavalry.
5. If your infantry beat their infantry and your cavalry was still around then
6. your cavalry could rout their infantry who would otherwise
7. retreat and join up with their beaten cavalry
8. to fight another day.

The key step was always (4) because while mounted lancers were as fearsome as tanks, neither can inflict decisive damage wandering unsupported around the countryside. They might cause an awful lot of mayhem but unless the enemy has already mentally given up, he can wait until the hay or the petrol runs out. There is precious little a tank can do to dug-in troops armed with the most basic of anti-tank weapons.

Post-cavalry, the central battlefield problem is that tanks are at a great disadvantage when up against anti-tank guns. The gun is specifically designed to destroy tanks while the tank is designed to do all manner of tasks which do not primarily include destroying anti-tank guns. Tanks have to move around, restricting the size of their main armament and making them highly visible; anti-tank guns can be any size and will be hidden, preferably on the reverse slope. Tanks' most important duty is to take on other tanks so they must have high velocity, flat trajectory, armour-piercing guns; taking out an anti-tank gun is best achieved with a low velocity, arcing trajectory, high explosive gun. A tank can carry both types of ammunition but not both types of gun.

Early British tanks did not even carry both types of ammunition but they eventually turned to the Grant tank which did have both types of gun: a smallish one in the turret and a biggish one bolted to the chassis. Unfortunately they discovered, as the French had discovered with their Char B, the gun in the turret was too small to take out another tank and to train the big one involved stopping your tank, manoeuvring it around, lining it up on the other tank that had in the meantime destroyed your tank. The two-gun solution has not been proceeded with.

Which, said the theorists, is exactly why tanks are re-quired *en masse*, so the advancing side can accept some losses but the anti-tank gun line will be rolled over. This is fair enough, depending on your definition of 'some losses', but does not solve the next problem: tanks are inherently expensive, anti-tank mines and bazookas (and missiles from helicopter gunships for that matter) are inherently cheap. Assuming the defenders stay in place—if necessary allowing tanks to roll over them and charge off *en masse* into the interior—they will convert 'some losses' into 'all lost' as the unsupported tanks wander around making what they can of a landscape perforated with mines, baz-ookas and helicopter gunships. Plus more anti-tank guns since they are relatively cheap as well. What to do? Join the navy?

The Germans used logic. They dispensed with panzer divisions, except as administrative units, and started dis-tributing their tanks in penny packets. Maybe they had no choice given their chronic shortage of tanks but pro forma they went back to the old ways when for thousands of years 'all arms' were used on the battlefield—a bit of this mixed in with a bit of that. Penny packets in fact. The Wehrmacht did not, despite occupying Crete, actually use Cretan slingers mixed in with their phalanxes, but they did dispense with their phalanxes which are excellent if the other side turns up with one as well and it's their shove against your shove, but Heaven help you if it's Attila the Hun.

The quality of the tanks makes a difference to these calcul-ations. Before the war the British had got it into their heads that it was essential for tanks to be transportable by rail. This was clearly a consideration for Germany whose tanks might need to be shuttled rapidly from front to front, maybe also for countries in the direct firing line such as France or Russia with a need to get tanks rapidly into action. The only obvious gain for Britain, whose tanks would be fighting overseas, was to cut transport costs from factory to port.

But the British love their railways so they built their tanks to fit them. The reason they love their railways is that they invented them, making British railways the oldest in the world and therefore having the narrowest loading gauge in the world which meant British tanks had to be the narrowest in the world which meant getting a decent gun on them meant they had to be the highest in the world, presenting the most conspicuous silhouette to enemy gunners in the world, but also the narrowest tracks in the world leading to the worst speed, manoeuvrability and reliability in the world, the smallest gun to weight ratio in the world and the lowest net cost of delivery from factory to port in the world.

Once the lessons of this policy had been learned on the battlefield the British resolved to buy American and ran into a different problem. While the British were inventing and falling in love with their railways, their fellow WASPs had been inventing and falling in love with mass production, and were just as mesmerised by this innovation when it came to designing and building tanks. To maximise mass production a minimum of change to the specification of the end product is required: you can have any colour you want so long as it is a matt grey-green Mark I Sherman.

The trouble with this policy is that, as battlefield lessons sink in and new countermeasures are dreamt up by the enemy, what is soon required of *any* piece of military hardware is a Mark II, a Mark II (a), a Mark II (a) Special and before you know it, a Mark III. Every time there is a change in specification the production line has to be halted, new machinery installed, workers retrained and the numbers going out the door go down and down and down. It's a production engineer's worst nightmare. So the Americans (and the British) always turned up for battle in matt grey-green Mark I Shermans.

This was not all bad because when they turned up for battle in Normandy in 1944 they could put ten 1941-era Sherman tanks up against one German 1943-era Mark V Panther. The Panther might knock out nine of the Shermans but the tenth would get him and the Anglo-American tide could flow on. Possibly five 1943-era Shermans would have been better, the brewed-up tank crews might have thought so, but the tide flowed on with or without them. The British did think it worth tinkering with their quota of Shermans by putting a Panther-busting seventeen-pounder gun on a Sherman chassis but they had to pay the production price and there were never enough of them to make a difference. One of them got Michael Wittman (q.v.) though.

There were enough tanks ranged against each other in Normandy to thoroughly test out the *en masse or penny packets* theory. The Germans created special Abteilungs of a mere handful of tanks and attached them to stretches of threatened perimeter. The Germans did technically have panzer regiments, panzer divisions, even panzer armies, but the reality was their tanks had to be distributed in penny packets, not solely because of their scarcity, but because the incessant attentions of Allied tank-busting planes made it essential. Besides it worked a treat. Hitler, a 1940 throw-back, insisted that panzer regiments, panzer divisions, even panzer armies be laboriously reconstituted for some operation or other but these were always colossal failures.

The Anglo-Americans were 1918 throwbacks and massed their tanks in great numbers to advance in tight formations against prepared German gun lines. Armies never talk to navies which is a shame because any sailor could have told them this is called 'crossing your own T' and has been studiously avoided since the seventeenth century. The advancing column can only engage with its leading units but the advanced-upon line can fire back with everything it's got.

This dogged will to lose on the part of the Anglo-Americans was the more surprising because the Allied army commander was Bernard Montgomery who had reached his exalted position by doing the complete opposite in all his previous battles. Montgomery's first independent command was at Alam Halfa in the Western desert in 1942 where he had arrived with the inestimable advantage of being an infantryman with no experience of how tanks are supposed to be used on the modern battlefield. He carefully dug in his guns, banished tanks to the rear and halted Rommel's onrushing armoured columns with ease.

Next, at Alamein, he showed he understood the situation perfectly by eschewing massed tanks for the initial break-in battle, eschewing them again when that did not work, eschewing them again when switching to another break-in battle on the northern flank, and eschewing them again for the break-out when that was successful. He only let loose the tanks, in penny packets, for the pursuit of the rapidly retreating enemy. This policy was roundly condemned by Churchill, tank generals and historians who with one voice pointed out the German and Italian forces lived to fight another day. 'And British tanks lived to fight another day,' Montgomery probably thought, remembering what had happened on every other occasion British tanks had charged headlong en masse following a local success.

He understood the value of providing opponents with golden bridges and repeated the formula at the Mareth Lines in Tunisia in 1943. The Mareth Lines are, I think, unique in the annals of war in being built by the French to defend against the Italians but used exclusively by Italians to defend against (Free) French. Montgomery comfortably stopped Rommel's tank advance with guns then conducted his own advance using infantry and artillery, sending his tanks off on a wide outflanking manoeuvre far away from the battlefield. It is true Monty's tactics meant the Axis were forever fighting another day but wasn't that the point of the Mediterranean strategy? To tie up German troops that could more profitably be used in Europe? The Axis ended up surrendering a quarter of a million men at Tunis when the golden bridges ran out. Anglo-American losses were more from venereal disease.

As soon as Montgomery got to Normandy in 1944, he forgot all this. Why? One has to suppose that with Detroit on his side, and captious Americans *by* his side, he figured he could afford to lose tanks in more or less any number in exchange for the break-out. The difficulty was that, as a British soldier, he actually answered to Britain and by this stage of the war *Brit* rhymed with *frit*. After quite modest casualties each of his tank offensives was called off with no break-out in sight. This served British interests rather well: leave it to the Americans and the Russians who had yet to learn the benefits of frit.

Which reminds me, the battle we tank buffs most wanted to see was between the Americans and the Russians across the ideal tank country of the north German plain. But they wouldn't play ball. Frit, I expect. Not that we tank buffs would have finally got our answer to *en masse or penny packets* because the Russians would have won in a canter whichever method they used.

* * *

18   Michael Wittman vs The British Empire

The British army reached its fighting peak during the Normandy campaign of June 1944, being composed of veterans from the Western Desert or troops trained for a year or more with this very campaign in mind. They were superbly equipped on the ground, had overwhelming support from the air and even the navy was lobbing in fifteen-inch shells.

The position the army found itself in, after the successful landings and lodgement, presented no undue complications. The Germans held a well-organised perimeter which the British had to break through and they could do so at a time and a place of their own choosing—the kind of set-piece battle their commander, Montgomery, specialised in. He painstakingly assembled a considerable preponderance of armour, mobile infantry, artillery and tactical aircraft at the vital point, spearheaded by his most renowned formation, the 7th Armoured Division, the 'Desert Rats'. Complete surprise was achieved, another Montgomery speciality, and the British made a good start. The Desert Rats were quickly in possession of their first day's objective, the strategically important village of Villers-Bocage.

German tactical doctrine was that whenever there was a break in the line an immediate counter-attack had to be launched to seal the breach. Accordingly, three Tiger tanks were sent to investigate the situation in Villers-Bocage. After a cautious observation their commander, Captain Michael Wittmann, ordered two of the tanks to report back while he himself would make what might be called a 'reconnaissance in force'. The first thing he noted was that

British reinforcements, in the form of an armoured column, were moving up towards Villers-Bocage. The British were in a long row of single line transport which, here in the 'bocage country', was seemingly unavoidable. The *bocage* is a Norman form of land use in which very small fields are surrounded by tall hedges impenetrable to anything short of a bulldozer. In between the hedges are narrow sunken lanes along one of which the British column was advancing. Wittmann used the Tiger's 88mm gun to knock out the first and last vehicles in the column, trapping the entire unit which he then destroyed one by one. After this he drove around using essentially the same technique wherever he spotted British forces advancing towards the village.

The British had first been made aware of the effectiveness of the 88mm in France in 1940 when the Germans discovered that what they thought they had brought along as an anti-aircraft weapon was the only gun that could make a dent in British Matilda tanks. They took the lesson on board and adopted the 88, in the anti-tank role, for the campaigns in the Western Desert, to be used against British tanks armed with 37, 50 or 75 mm guns. The British never quite worked out how to deal with this situation though they had the comparable 3.7 inch gun. This for some reason had to be pointed upwards in the anti-aircraft role, so the British only advanced when their excellent tactical aircraft and artillery had eliminated the 88's.

Viewing Wittman's carnage, the British concluded that somehow the Germans had created a new gun line of 88's but as the gun line did not exist, it proved impossible on this occasion to eliminate it with either aircraft or artillery. British HQ reluctantly ordered the Desert Rats to withdraw from the village and, since British tactical doctrine was that neighbouring units had to fall back to 'maintain the integrity of the line', the other British units taking part had to withdraw to their starting positions as well. The Villers-Bocage offensive was over.

*   *   *

19 Aces High

The concept of the 'ace' emerged in the First World War when the French, anxious to introduce an element of Gallic knight-errantry into the industrial charnel house, began publicising the exploits of pilots who had shot down a lot of enemy aircraft. You actually kept score! The Germans adopted *le sport* with relish though the British thought it showing off and initially refused to take part. But before long it became a serious business for everyone because the home front took it very much to heart and modern war is all about the home front. Not surprisingly the concept was embraced from the outset of the Second World War.

The French got knocked out before they could acquire aces and the British, after the Battle of Britain, were handicapped by a dearth of German planes. An Irish rugby international did hold the individual world record for destroying enemy aircraft but he was using a machine gun mounted on an SAS jeep so was disqualified for unsportsmanlike conduct.

The Americans had a mixed record. Japanese planes were so flimsy they could be despatched with a single incendiary bullet and ace status (five kills in their system) could be gained in an afternoon. German planes were made of sterner stuff. Inspection of enemy records after the war showed a consistent pattern: for every ten German planes shot down according to the Americans, the German record-keepers could only find one. In the Korean War American pilots shot down ten enemy planes for every one of their own though as we do not yet have access to the enemy's records it could have been more. They were often

77

up against Russian pilots but in the Second World War the Soviets only gave snipers the Stakhanovite treatment.

Despite the Second War being even more a mass production business than the First, it was found that aces were not just simple morale boosters—they could actually determine whole campaigns. The earliest example of this phenomenon was the U-boat ace. Certainly these grizzled, weatherbeaten figures were lionised by the German media, but in truth a tiny number of submarine commanders were responsible for a disproportionate amount of Allied shipping losses. However, of their nature, aces do not last indefinitely and, one by one, as 'die Alte' fell, so too did the rate of Allied sinkings. Dönitz, the U-boat chief, tried to manufacture aces by offering Iron Crosses for such-and-such tonnage of ships sunk but it soon became evident that this new breed of U-boat commanders, despite being more Nazified than the old Kriegsmarine skippers, were not pressing in for the kill with quite the determination of their illustrious predecessors. Not too much comfort should be taken from this—the best fighting unit produced by the war was the Hitler Youth division of the Waffen SS. Little aces all.

Dönitz never solved the problem and neither did the Americans when they in turn unleashed their fabulous submarines on the woefully underprepared Japanese. A handful of captains sank ship after ship, other captains came home again and again without so much as loosing off a torpedo. Not that either American or German torpedoes were much good. It is a weirdness of war that nations bend their every will to produce the very best in delivery systems but leave that which is to be delivered to obscure wunderkinds in secret outstations, only to be thoroughly disconcerted when they do not work as advertised. World

War Three will be decided by a weapons system (a nuke on the end of a missile) that has never *once* been tested in practice. I'm a Londoner, let me know how it turned out.

There were also tank aces. Or to be more accurate there were German tank aces since no British, American or Russian tank commander could hope to destroy a sufficient number of superior German tanks (and doctrine) to qualify for ace-hood. One was a good score for them. But here's a strange thing. The whole point of the ace system is that individuals must emerge via some kind of single combat in dangerous circumstances and for a tank ace that requires taking on head to head another tank or self-propelled anti-tank gun. If you are an ace and if you are in a German tank, the odds on each separate occasion will presumably be better than fifty-fifty but even so how is it possible for, say, the aforementioned Michael Wittman to win 138 times against other tanks and 132 times against self-propelled guns? This defies even Bayesian logic.

The Japanese had their air aces—an astonishingly large number if US accounts of their air battles are taken at face value—but liked to credit the unit rather than the man. Though, by a quirk of contemporary technology, their aces could have brought them victory. The Pacific War surely holds the record for largest area vis à vis smallest amount of military hardware; also the record for smallest number of individuals vis à vis largest possible outcome. Whoever's fleet, American or Japanese, was superior would decide that outcome; whoever's fleet was superior would be decided by a handful of aircraft carriers; whoever's aircraft carriers were superior would be decided by a handful of carrier pilots.

As is usually the case in Great Power conflict, the two sides were remarkably well matched at the outset—if they

79

had not been, one side or the other would have declined to fight. In January 1942 (Pearl Harbour turned out to be irrelevant, the American carriers being away on exercise) each side had roughly the same number and quality of carriers, roughly the same number and quality of planes, roughly the same number and quality of pilots. The victor would be determined by two factors arising from the respective national character of the combatants. That is why we have wars in the first place, no other method of resolving disputes quite does the job.

The Japanese despised defensive measures—Bushido, Banzai and all that—so they seldom prepared for being attacked as opposed to doing the attacking. When Japanese carriers *were* attacked, they did not last long. America by contrast cosseted its sailors as if every last one's mother would write to her congressman if anything untoward happened to her boy, so American carriers were built to survive most everything hurled at them. The other factor was that the sneaky Americans were reading the honourable Japanese' codes so the Americans could arrange a naval battle whenever and wherever it suited them. It suited them in the Coral Sea in May 1942 (one carrier lost by each side) and at Midway in June (four Japanese carriers lost to one American). With her carriers so diminished, Japan had to retreat from island to island until she ran out of islands.

Japanese carrier pilots were already the cream of the national crop, so where do the 'aces' come in? The technology of the time dictated the sequence of events in Pacific naval battles. As the fleets steamed towards each other, the battle would start with, say, sixty torpedo and dive bombers escorted by a similar number of fighters setting out from the Japanese carriers towards the US fleet. Some will get lost, some will be intercepted by US fighters, some will be shot down by anti-aircraft fire, most will deliver a bomb or a torpedo on the American carriers. The great majority will miss and those few that hit will be dealt with by the matchless American damage control parties. The US carriers will plough on, bloodied but unbowed. Meanwhile they will have sent off similar forces to attack the Japanese carriers with similar results except Japanese carriers did not have matchless damage control and mostly did not survive the few bombs and torpedoes that hit them. Bereft of carriers the rest of the Japanese battle fleet would have to retreat, unbloodied but bowed.

Unbeknownst to the Japanese, they had a weapon that could cut through all this. Kamikaze attacks are widely regarded as both desperate and futile which was indeed the case in 1944 when the Japanese got round to adopting the tactic. The Americans by then had such a superiority that few kamikazes survived the serried defences and those that did caused damage that was serious but not consequential. If the policy had been adopted at the Battle of Midway in 1942 things would have been quite different because conditions in 1942 were quite different. By war's end the USA had a hundred aircraft carriers but there is no doubt that kamikaze attacks in 1942 would have eliminated *all* operational US carriers. Cream-of-the-crop 1942 Japanese navy pilots could, unlike hastily trained 1944 kamikazes, find and identify their targets, they could survive the feeble defences of a 1942 US task force and they could virtually guarantee to hit an American carrier if, as it were, they accompanied their bombs all the way down. Damage control would not have saved a single carrier under such circumstances. Why didn't the Japanese use such a war-altering policy in 1942? It was because, by

Japanese standards, the carrier pilots *were* aces. The cream of the crop. The idea of deliberately sacrificing them was unthinkable. The fact they were lost anyway when the carriers went down never entered into their calculations.

Ironically, the potentially most significant aces of all were produced by Italy, otherwise a nation of military incompetence beyond the measure of man. The Italians had come up with the idea of midget submarines and used them to sink the two British battleships of the Mediterranean fleet in Alexandria harbour. The strategic importance of the operation lay in its timing, a few days after Pearl Harbour, with the world on a knife edge. Once these six individuals had put the *Valiant* and *Queen Elizabeth* out of commission, the Italian battle fleet could have forced the British, now without any battleships at all, from the Mediterranean, rendering the entire southern Axis theatre unnecessary. This in turn would have freed up the resources vital for the decisive Russian campaigns of 1942. But it wasn't to be. Those crafty Inglese jacked up their two capital ships so it looked for all the world as if they were battle ready and when up against the Italians, a 'fleet in being' is all that is required.

What holds true for every nation is that aces are born and not made. There seems no way of knowing ahead of time whether a given individual will cut it, much less emerge as an ace. The skills (and courage) demanded cannot be acquired whether by training or by experience— they have to reveal themselves in action. The Americans, who like to measure this sort of thing and get plenty of opportunities to do so, have consistently found, no matter how fierce the fire fight and no matter how elite the unit, only ten per cent or so of weapons have actually been fired. This is the more surprising given that modern armed forces are ten per cent front-line and ninety per cent rear echelon. Nobody, it seems, knows how to select the right ten per cent. A small mercy.

*   *   *

20 Airmindedness

When aircraft attack ground forces

1. individual soldiers are pretty much immune
2. stationary tanks, guns, vehicles etc are pretty much immune
3. moving tanks, guns, vehicles etc at night are pretty much immune
4. moving tanks, guns, vehicles etc during the day are at some risk.

This presupposes the ground troops have taken minor precautions but it does not presuppose anything about the technology available to either side, nor the kind of terrain in which the attacks are being carried out. These end results were as valid in the Second World War as they might be today if, for the sake of argument, the best tactical air forces in the world (perhaps a combination of American, Russian and British) were operating in really favourable terrain (maybe a desert) and bombing people who don't even have the sense to wear helmets (possibly an ad hoc bunch of rag-tag stumblebums with towels round their heads).

Nevertheless the tactic can be effective. If the ground troops lack the esprit de corps of ISIS it does not matter what degree of harm the planes can inflict, the ground troops might still cut and run. British soldiers in the Second World War were prone to do this. 'Prone' being something of an understatement if we are to believe Evelyn Waugh's account of the Crete campaign in the *Sword of Honour* trilogy, the finest piece of military writing in English literature. He was there so I am inclined to believe him, fiction or no.

This proclivity was relatively unimportant as the French and Norwegian campaigns of 1940 were doomed anyway and in North Africa the Law of Big Battalions ultimately took effect—the British won as soon as they had over-whelming superiority on land *and* in the air. In all campaigns thereafter German planes ceased to bother British ground troops because they were conspicuous by their absence. Just three English infantry divisions in the Norm-andy battles for example.

The Americans to a degree shared the tendency and this had a major bearing on Allied planning: if it scares the be-jesus out of our lads, why don't we do it to theirs? The first experiment was at Cassino in 1943. The British and Amer-icans were being held up south of Rome which was deeply irritating because this was the major fighting front for these two martial nations whereas for the Germans it was a side-show. There was a terrific road going straight through to Rome but to get onto it the town of Cassino had to be captured, plus the heights above it.

Cassino is a small and unremarkable place surrounded by a fair amount of open ground favourable for tanks, mobile infantry, concentrated artillery and all the things the Allies had in abundance and the Germans did not. For six months the Allies tried various ways to get the Ger-mans to recognise they didn't stand a chance, then there was a pause while both sides reflected on their respective situations. The Germans understood the strategic signific-ance of Cassino and put in their best soldiers, paratroopers fighting in the infantry role. The Anglo-Americans under-stood it too and put up *their* best troops, New Zealanders fighting in any role except against paratroopers, as they had demonstrated in Crete. (The Australians, the *very* best Allied soldiers, had been sent off to the Pacific at the behest of their government, to be ignored by MacArthur because they had their own public relations people.)

All was ready but the Allied high command decided, to be on the safe side, they would ask their air forces to bomb the German garrison in Cassino to oblivion. No harm was done to the paratroopers but Cassino itself was reduced to a pile of smoking ruins. This was unfortunate because fighting in built-up areas is best done by the infantry 'mouseholing' their way through the houses with tank support from the streets and neither is feasible when houses and streets have been bombed to oblivion. The defenders found this new urban landscape more to their liking, bomb craters and masonry heaps giving them an infinite supply of strongpoints. In the end the New Zealanders had to give up and the Allies had to find a new stratagem.

Why not bomb *Monte* Cassino, the famous monastery that overlooked the town? The whole world, from the Pope downwards, was assuring them the Germans had agreed not to use it for any purpose (and weren't) but it was flattened anyway whereupon the Germans moved into the ruins and a splendid observation post and defensive redoubt it made too.

Eventually, and without air support, the least regarded of the Allies, the Free French, used their least regarded soldiers, Algerian *goumiers*, to solve the problem by hopping along the flanking peaks on the other side of the road, thus forcing the Germans in the valley to withdraw. Fairly standard tactics except for armies wedded to mechanismo. A few weeks later the Allies were in Rome and the goumiers returned to obscurity until 1958 when it was the turn of French paratroopers in Algeria to learn the lesson all over again.

Nevertheless this new 'carpet bombing' idea had its supporters. The British and American tactical air forces liked it because it was exactly the kind of not-very-precise but just-precise-enough technique they were now very good at. The troops liked it because seeing the enemy being plastered cheered them up immensely before going over the top. The brass liked it because it made for spectacular newsreel evidence that 'something was being done'. So the next time the main Allied effort was being held up indefinitely by scratch German forces it was wheeled out again.

This was in Normandy where the city of Caen, scheduled for capture on D-Day , was still in German hands six weeks later, enraging everyone except the ground commander, Montgomery, who cheerfully claimed the campaign was going exactly to plan. This enraged everyone even more so he resolved 'something must be done' and ordered the biggest carpet bombing exercise thus far to be followed by the biggest tank assault thus far. Lessons had been learned and it was not Caen itself that was plastered (that came later) but the German positions in open country to the east of the city. Not much damage was done to German troops or equipment but enormous craters appeared everywhere, uprooted trees blocked all routes and village crossroads were blown to smithereens. The open country to the east of Caen was no longer open. Unable to advance rapidly or manoeuvre freely, the tanks were picked off in their hundreds by German guns and the British offensive petered out.

Seeing this, the Americans decided to put on their own show and started carpet bombing their sector. Literally— they bombed their own troops—but the Yanks had more stickability than the Brits and kept hammering away until the breakthrough was achieved and it was safe for General Patton to conduct the Allied armies across France.

I see from the evening news Raqqa is being bombed yet again. No wait, late breaking news, Raqqa has just fallen to some other bunch of towel-heads. Wearing American helmets, I see.

*   *   *

21 The Wooden Walls of England

The most famous bomber of the Second World War was the B-17 Flying Fortress. Then and now this aircraft is revered as the super-weapon of its era, a reputation that may have more to do with it being built up the road from Hollywood, because the B-17 was a truly awful aeroplane.

As a heavy bomber it had some fundamental flaws, the chief of which was a lack of bombs. Two tons was typical for a German target. To get those two tons there required ten people, and aircrew were among the most extensively trained personnel of the war. Lots of aircrew had to be trained because each ten-man batch was soon lost due to a strange idea held by the B-17's designers. Ever since air combat began in the First World War fighters could always shoot down bombers. This is an application of a rule of war that affects all armament design, in this case that fighters are designed to shoot down bombers, bombers are not designed to shoot down fighters.

The Americans had every opportunity to observe whether the rule still held because the world's premier air forces, the RAF and the Luftwaffe, had been testing it out for two whole years, and had found that it did. But Americans—and in many ways it is an admirable trait—believe they can always stick it to the old world and they responded by putting more and more machine guns onto the B-17 (hence the large crew and the small bombload) and launched them off to take on the German fighters (hence the large losses).

The other lesson that everybody except the Americans had learnt was that precision bombing by large formations was not possible. Both the RAF and the Luftwaffe had acquired the technology for mainly finding the right city but that was the limit of 'precision'. The Americans regarded this as more European pussyfooting—they had the Norden bombsight which could 'put a bomb in a pickle barrel'. And so it could, in the Arizona desert. When the Americans had to bomb German pickle barrels they discovered they could achieve no more and no less accuracy than anyone else.

It takes a lot to disabuse an American military panjandrum so the B-17s were sent off time and again in search of things nobody else could find—what the British panjandrum 'Bomber' Harris dismissed as 'panacea targets'—culminating in a series of raids on the ball bearing plants at Schweinfurt. It was true, if enough B-17s were sent to bomb Schweinfurt, then ball bearing factories, of which Schweinfurt was full, might be hit along with everything else. And they were! Entire ball bearing factories were reduced to rubble and the Americans had the aerial reconnaissance photographs to prove it.

The Germans were forced to wheel out their machine tools, put up some tarpaulin and start making al fresco ball bearings. The factories, being deep in the heart of Germany, meant the B-17s now had to get home through the ranks of alerted enemy fighters armed with cannons and a range of five hundred yards, and only their machine guns with half that range to fend them off. It was a race against time. Would the Americans run out of B-17s before the Germans ran out of tarpaulin?

The Americans never solved this problem (until the Germans ran out of fighters) but the British were conducting their own experiments. Their equivalent of the B-17 was the Lancaster (and the Halifax) designed a generation after the mid-thirties' Fortress and incorporating the lessons gained from years of strategic bombing. One thing learned was that effective bombers are inordinately expensive to produce. Another lesson, acquired from being strategically *bombed*, was that an inordinate number of them would be required to dent Germany's war economy. The Luftwaffe, whisper it, had barely scratched their own.

Indeed, being strategically bombed could be positively beneficial. The flattening of Red Clydeside, for example, had converted several thousand bolshie shipbuilders from stay-at-home strikers to patriots with only the shipyards to call home. Productivity soared when the shipyards were back in full working order, a good twenty-four hours after the Germans had departed, though it took a deal longer to get the Glasgow housing stock back in working order. That took more like twenty-four years. The moral of the story? Vote Conservative.

Four thousand Lancasters would be needed, the statisticians reckoned, to avoid the same unintended consequence in Germany. Nothing approaching this number was ever achieved because the Lancasters were being shot down in such Fortress-style proportions that just replacing them was warping the British war economy. Not the German one, which reached its peak of production in the autumn of 1944. That was hardly the point. The Anglo-Americans were having such a minor effect on Germany anywhere at this stage of the war that whatever damage was being done can be considered a reasonable use of their resources. Plus it was diverting German heavy artillery and fighter planes from the Eastern front where the damage *was* being done.

The Allied bombing campaign may or may not have been an error but using B-17s and Lancasters to conduct it was.

The correct solution lay close at hand and was already in mass production. Mosquitoes could carry comparable bombloads to Fortresses over Germany but were very much cheaper to build. Being made from non-strategic wood and glue and built by furniture-makers with no furniture to make in Austerity Britain, they warped few war industries. Nor did Mosquitoes require many expensively trained aircrew because there were only two of them and they seldom needed replacing on account of the Wooden Wonder flying faster than German fighters and higher than German flak.

Concentrating on Mosquitoes—and from early in the war the British on their own were producing more aircraft of every kind than the Germans—would have meant many thousands of bombers over Germany. What that would have done for the German war effort is uncertain but it would have done wonders for the British war effort. And if the USA had been building Mosquitoes too? Tens of thousands of bombers and even German morale might have cracked.

Why didn't any of this happen? Why did the air forces not avail themselves of this logical and accessible solution? We can acquit the Americans who would clearly prefer tens of thousands of their sons dying than be seen relying on British technology, but the British had their own rationale. The RAF had been busying itself building bigger and bigger bombers ever since the First World War *and* converting them from wood to metal, so there was to be no going back as far the airmen were concerned. Or coming back for so many of them.

*　　　*　　　*

22 Beacon of Light

Leslie Hore-Belisha, the British minister in charge of the army when war broke out, has a permanent place in the lexicon because earlier in his career he gave us the Belisha beacon. He has another claim to fame as the subject of the best royal joke of the war. It is autumn 1939 and the Prime Minister is having his weekly audience with the King:

> **Neville Chamberlain:** We're sending Hore-Belisha
>   over for talks with the French.
> **George VI:** Surely a case of coals to Newcastle.
> **Chamberlain:** I don't follow you, Sir.
> **George VI:** Sending a Hore to Paris.

The 'Phoney War' (or the 'Bore War' as the fun-loving British called it) lasted from the fall of Poland in September 1939 until the invasion of Norway in April 1940. It is not dealt with in detail by historians for the understandable reason that not much fighting was going on and the diplomatic wranglings were soon rendered moot. This is presumably why one mysterious episode has gone underreported. In January 1940 Hore-Belisha suddenly resigned. He was offered a couple of other cabinet posts but opted to return to the backbenches.

His resignation was obviously a sacking by Chamberlain and the reason for it is murky. In Churchill's official biography it is implied, but not explicitly stated, that Hore-Belisha's removal was demanded by Lord Gort, C-in-C of the British army in France, supported by his two corps commanders. Either he went or they went. Given the situation, with a German attack expected at any time, it was

unrealistic to accept the resignation of all three field commanders, so it was Hore-Belisha that had to go. A cabinet
reshuffle had been engineered by the British Army, the
nearest thing to a military coup in recent British history.
Not very near to be sure, and something similar had occurred in the Great War, but even so one would think the
incident worthy of a book, maybe a chapter in a book,
more anyway than the customary paragraph. God knows
there are entire tomes devoted to incidents in the war that
scarcely rate a footnote.

There was a back story, two back stories. Hore-Belisha
had been appointed War Minister in 1937 and had energet-
ically set about the much needed modernising of the army,
and to the loud complaints of the army. Nevertheless
civilian authority had prevailed and the soldiers were
shoved kicking and squealing into the nineteen-twenties.
Hore-Belisha was a Jew, an archetypal 'pushy' Jew, and
there was anti-Semitic talk. This was probably not all that
significant, anti-Semitic talk being quite open among the
higher rungs of British society at the time. Unless it was—
caste signalling among the British ruling elite can be hard
to interpret—but suffice to say Hore-Belisha's career pros-
pered until the events of January 1940.

Churchill (a notable pro-Semite, if that is the term) had
an equivocal role in the sacking. In a letter to Hore-Belisha
he claimed to know nothing of his dismissal but did hint
that he approved of the move. Churchill's own position
was equivocal. As First Lord of the Admiralty he was technically at the same cabinet rank as Hore-Belisha himself,
which was not very high. Being the administrative head of
an armed service is not a top job in the British system,
even in wartime. Yet Churchill was unashamedly acting as
a kind of prime minister-in-waiting, not only dominating

cabinet discussions (nobody could shut him up) but constantly launching himself on 'fact-finding tours' to northern France where there were no ships but there was the frontline strength of the British army. Churchill was certainly in deepest cahoots with Gort and his relationship with the two dissident corps commanders was also close. One of them, Alanbrooke, became Churchill's right-hand man during the war; the other, Pownall, was his right-hand man after the war, helping out with the epic *Second World War* which earned Churchill a Nobel Prize. For Literature! There's hope for us all.

After his departure from office Hore-Belisha had, in the popular phrase, 'an interesting war'. When Churchill constructed his Grand Coalition in May 1940 there was no official opposition but the House of Commons abhors a vacuum and gradually an anti-government grouping emerged, consisting of the far left (especially after the Soviet Union entered the war), the far right (unreconciled Chamberlainites) and the resentful centre (Liberals awaiting the second coming). Being unofficial, leadership devolved onto forceful individuals with their own personal reasons for malcontent: Manny Shinwell (insulted at not being given a suitably important job), Nye Bevan (folk memories of Churchill at Tonypandy), and Hore-Belisha himself who gradually took on the mantle of de facto Leader of the Opposition.

Collectively they were hopeless, whether as parliamentary tacticians or as tribunes of the people, but they proved to be of great use to Churchill because they made excellent lightning rods for public impatience with the seemingly unending military failures. They could articulate popular discontent without being able to do anything about it. It is the British way and serves us well. Or serves us right.

23 Jews In High Places

When fighting a war against an opponent who is virulently anti-Semitic, Jews and Jewishness become factors in that war. Nowadays we are virulently *anti*-anti-Semitic, so this can get overlooked.

Take by way of example the sacking of Hore-Belisha in January 1940. Hore-Belisha's official title, Secretary of State for War, was unfortunate because though this grand-sounding position is not in reality of the highest, it may be perceived otherwise by those lacking a working knowledge of British executive appellation practices. Having a Jewish holder of the post is of little consequence in Britain, there are normally Jews at the top of British governments in war as well as peace—Herbert Samuel, Rufus Isaacs and Edwin Montagu were cabinet ministers in the First War. Jews could be found in influential positions in *German* governments both under Bismarck and during Weimar, but in 1939 the British having a Jewish 'minister for war' was a propaganda gift for Goebbels. It would have been wholly proper on these grounds alone for the British to quietly shift Hore-Belisha to a less sensitive post, though this seems not to have been a factor when he was.

But there is another reason. Goebbels was right! Jews may not be the best people to conduct wars against virulently anti-Semitic opponents. A member of a government is supposed to be framing policy in accordance with the interests of the country and while we all know in practice they are up to lots of other things—lining their own pockets, favouring their own class and so forth—it is still a job requirement that they 'benefit the country'. As far as is known Jews are no different from anyone else—lining their own pockets, favouring their own class and so forth—but in the unique circumstance of a war against a virulently anti-Semitic opponent, it is difficult to imagine that a Jewish minister's judgement would be solely and exclusively predicated on the service of his country.

Hore-Belisha was not senior enough and not in office long enough to be important, unlike Morgenthau in the United States. The Jewish Henry Morgenthau (I put it like that because for some reason Americans do not like the word 'Jew') was Roosevelt's Secretary of the Treasury, an appropriate post one might think, given standard stereotyping. But this would be wrong, the job normally went to a different stereotype, a scion of a traditional WASP dynasty, of which Roosevelt himself was a prime example. Nor would the Secretary of the Treasury ordinarily be framing foreign policy but in 1940 Morgenthau was instrumental in pushing the ultra-nervous Roosevelt into overt military support for Britain. This cannot be understood by discounting his Jewishness.

As events transpired this was in *America's* interest, but in 1944 Morgenthau came up with the Morgenthau Plan which, as events transpired, was not in America's interest. The Plan proposed that Germany be to all intents and purposes de-industrialised and broken up into smaller states. A not unreasonable proposition given recent history, and the Plan was seriously considered in both America and Britain. However, it was decisively rejected and the opposite policy pursued when the Marshall Plan and various British initiatives swiftly restored Germany, *West* Germany, to the ranks of military and industrial powers.

Morgenthau was almost certainly in this instance acting as a Jewish rather than as an 'American' cabinet minister. Goebbels made great play of this very point in 1944, and Goebbels like all the best propagandists spoke the truth whenever he could. (He spoiled a good case by claiming Roosevelt was a Jew.) If the Morgenthau Plan never came close to acceptance under Roosevelt, it might have been put into practice if, for instance, Morgenthau himself had been President. The Russians would have embraced it with enthusiasm and the British could not have opposed their two bigger rivals. The French would have shrugged, c'est la guerre, and been mightily relieved.

All pointlessly speculative of course but it raises the sub-Goebbelsian question, why have there been no Jewish presidents? Morgenthau might have been the first since his selection as running mate in the 1944 presidential election would have catapulted him into the top job on Roosevelt's death in April 1945. But that was not a realistic possibility in 1944 given that a Catholic only got elected in 1960 and a Mormon only ran in 2012. Plenty of atheists and nutjobs but Protestant atheists and nutjobs.

How do we compare with America? The British can point to the nineteenth-century Disraeli who, while more Jewish than Moses, was technically Church of England. The Americans can counterclaim with Barry Goldwater (Republican candidate, 1964) who was Jewish by any standard—again apart from being Church of England. 'Episcopalian' as they call it over there for marketing reasons. The British are moving faster now. Both Michael Howard and Ed Miliband have recently made it to the final without getting the spoon, though these two should come with a warning: their failure was only partly down to the unpopularity of their parties. They were viewed with suspicion by the British electorate, not for being Jewish specifically, but for being sort of archetypally Jewish—*Machiavel* and *Geek* subarchetypes respectively. It is hard to explain to outsiders but as somebody put it at the time, "Ed Miliband? Too Jewish. They should have chosen his brother."

Stop press. Bernie Sanders just won the New Hampshire primary. As Kirsty put it on *Newsnight*, "The first Jewish American ever to win a presidential primary." This was news to most of us. That Bernie Sanders was Jewish. But the prospect of his success in 2016 gave the Morgenthau Precedent a contemporary twist. In Britain Sanders would be more or less automatically anti-Israel (for us, ideology outweighs ethnicity) but for Sanders there are the two complications of growing up coevally with the State of Israel in a liberal, New York, Jewish household—I've read my Roth—and the Jewish political lobby. This latter rules out any overtly anti-Israel sentiments for people wanting to a) win the Presidency and b) rule effectively as President. On the other hand it is probably also true that *only* a Jewish President could take on a lobby that now extends far beyond Jews to embrace fundamentalist Christians, right-wing hawks, anti-Islamists, small towns, the rural heartland, the Bible belt, the wheat belt, the rust belt and both sides of the beltway.

If elected, a Jewish president might be able to perform a reverse-Morgenthau. It can scarcely be denied that America's pro-Israel stance is counterproductive in strictly Great Power terms. What was defensible during the Cold War, when so many Arab states were projections of Soviet power, is much less sensible when it is America's pro-Israel stance that is fuelling so much anti-Americanism, especially now Islamism has gone global. But this is to take a purely Great Power view. Americans are perfectly entitled to regard being in pole position for The Rapture as being worth the price of a disadvantageous foreign policy, though supporters of Israel ought not to bet the farm on the mercurial affections of nut jobs.

But it was not Sanders' Jewishness that marked him out for fear or favour, it was his *socialism*. Before 2016 the idea of a socialist in the White House would have everyone collapsed in mirth, yet it very nearly happened in the Second World War! If the fast-failing Roosevelt had died six months earlier than he in fact did, the left-of-Sanders Vice-President Henry Wallace would have become president. Though the idea of either Bernie Sanders or Henry Wallace being socialists would have everyone except Americans collapsed in mirth.

*   *   *

24 The Holocaust: For or Against?

Jeremy Bentham invented a useful philosophical device, the *felicific calculus*, by which to judge actions. You add up how much happiness an action produces, deduct how much unhappiness it causes and the net result determines whether it is a good decision or a bad one. Sounds simple, even obvious, but the *calculus* derives its usefulness from our inherent tendency to judge matters by how they affect us personally, not how they affect other people. We add up our own happiness and hope it doesn't affect anyone else's. They might stop us otherwise. On the big issues of the day we go a step further: if it is good for us personally, it is probably good for the world. That way we avoid hypocrisy and our world could not exist without hypocrisy.

On most people's reckoning one of the really bad things produced by the Second World War was the killing of the Jews. Not just bad, it is a benchmark of evil. But was it? Bentham insists we calculate, 'Was it bad for the world?' Sounds simple, even obvious, but we still have to run the numbers.

Minorities are a problem for all societies. 'Favouring one's own' is built in at the genetic level for all living things (to protect the genes) but genetic plurality also has to be built in (to protect the genes from a lack of diversity) so all species are 'societies' holding the ring for these two conflicting requirements. Human societies included, and as a general rule the more sophisticated a society the better able it is to maintain pluralities. Not the least shocking thing about the Nazi Holocaust (actually holocausts) is that

101

Germany 1933-45 was a very sophisticated society. In many ways the most sophisticated in human history at the time. Or, as the Nazis would put it, the most advanced when it comes to controlling the gene pool for the benefit of that society. Nor were they the only sophisticated people keen on 'eugenics'. It was all the rage.

Minorities have something to answer for as well. Since they are always unpopular they have a duty to 'fit in' if they know what's good for them. But they have genes of their own to protect. It can also pay to be a member of a minority, even a persecuted one. This is the *Etna Principle*: do you farm the rich slopes of the volcano knowing that sooner or later all you have, and occasionally you yourself, will be swept away in a cataclysm? Most minorities, given the choice, prefer membership of their minority and accept intolerance as their lot. Pressures to conform from the majority do not ordinarily reach the point of 'Conform or die' but German Nazis were a step-change worse than Spanish Inquisitors in not offering the choice.

It is difficult for us in the west, where anti-Semitism scarcely rises above a mild neurosis, to appreciate it was quite different in eastern Europe. At least it was when there *were* Jews in eastern Europe and when racism was not as verboten as it is today. Poles for instance detested the Jews on what might be called a national scale. As Jews made up a tenth of the population, that should read 'non-Jewish Poles detested Jewish Poles' but as non-Jewish Poles did not regard Jewish Poles as properly Polish, we'll leave it that way, especially as Jewish Poles often repaid the compliment with knobs on.

Serious, endemic, virulent anti-Semitism held sway anywhere there was a substantial Jewish minority—Russia,

Belarus, Ukraine, Latvia, Lithuania, Estonia, Hungary, Romania, Czechoslovakia, Austria. And Germany itself. All these populations, all these non-Jewish populations, shared the Polish view to a greater or lesser extent. Although it is unlikely that many of them, any of them, in 1939 would have voted for putting Jews in gas chambers, most people in eastern Europe were pleased—*are* pleased—the Jews are gone. When weighing the scales of the felicific calculus it has to be acknowledged, in raw numbers, more people benefited *directly* from the Holocaust than suffered from it.

But the calculus is capable of finer gradations than that. Let us take ours out for some Polish field trials in 1940. I'll ask the questions, you take notes and we'll take along an ethnologist, Herr Doktor SS Gruppenführer Müller, to make sure the questionnaire gets properly filled out. He's already arranged interviews with a couple of representative Poles.

> **Müller** (to Piotr): We are relocating your Jews.
> You can help yourself to anything left after
> they're gone.
> **Me:** Well, Piotr, how does that rate for you?
> Here's a chart to help you estimate.
> **Piotr:** I'll miss the cobbler but it's good riddance
> to the rest of them. The houses will be useful,
> we've still got kids living at home. Put me down
> for plus fifty points.
> **Me:** And that would be a general view?
> **Piotr:** All two thousand of us in this village, I can
> assure you of that.
> **Me** (to you): So that's fifty times two thousand.
> The event itself is a one-off but the benefits are

ongoing with diminishing marginal utility so we add an asterisk.

Müller: Some bad news, Izaak, your family is being relocated to Madagascar. The whole shtetl's going.

Izaak (consulting chart): Minus 250 I should say. Times two hundred. And add an asterisk, why don't you?

Time passes. We return to the village.

Müller: More bad news I'm afraid, Izaak. Madagascar turned out to be a non-starter. You and your wife are going to a labour camp. They're no picnics but we have every reason to keep you productive. And don't worry about the children, they will be adopted by good German families.

Izaak: Oy! Minus 1,000.

Time passes. We return to the village.

Müller: Yes, sorry, Izaak, back again but I promise this will be the final time. You and your wife will be sent to separate camps where you'll probably be worked to death. To be honest we don't much care, you won't be coming out either way. Your two children are, sorry to say, unproductive units and will be killed immediately. But humanely! We're not monsters.

Izaak: Minus 10,000 maybe?

Me (to you): No asterisk.

This is now called ethnic cleansing, a euphemism the SS wished it had thought up, but relocations of entire populations, including relocation by death, were a feature of the Second World War and its immediate aftermath. Some of these have actually turned out to be, um, beneficial. They have 'stuck'. Sudeten Germans are now just Germans, many of them buying holiday homes in the Sudetenland. Undoing these sweeping changes is not necessarily correct according to the felicific calculus. Has the world benefited from the Chechens being allowed back from their Stalinist banishment during the war and, if not, would you be brave enough to oppose their return? Some things are so fundamental we are prepared to pick up the tab.

Relocations vary in ways that are not always immediately apparent. Take the Madagascar solution that was semi-seriously canvassed. This would seem both appalling and impractical to us now but how would Izaak have responded given a choice between Madagascar and the Negev Desert? Some of Izaak's fellow-Ashkenazim were setting up kibbutzim in the Negev Desert but the British were being obstructive and would it really be sensible to swap a sea of Poles for a sea of Arabs? Why not become an honorary Frenchman in a sea of blacks? That is still essentially the position of the many Jews who went to South Africa. But the years roll by. It is now American Ashkenazim that spend their gap years on the kibbutz, Madagascar that proved to be no great shakes and South Africa that is still in the pending column. Untermenschen, übermenschen, wombling free.

We are circumspect about what counts as a holocaust, none of us wants the pain or the guilt, so we apply strict criteria before awarding the status. First and always is **number.** The body count has to be awe-inspiring. In the Second World War the Katyn massacre would not qualify because 'twelve thousand' is not sufficient even were we to factor in the other pits of Polish officer-dead. That is a war crime and no guilt is required. The numbers might reach the requisite totals were we to include the prodigious NKVD liquidations of Polish officer-types immediately after the war (anybody vaguely bourgeois qualified) but for some reason we do not count casual, grand scale mass murder as holocaustal. Interestingly, this is not even a war crime.

The second criterion is **intent**. Staying with Stalin, how do we evaluate the millions of Ukrainians, and others, who died in the famine following the collectivisation campaign of the early thirties? Did Stalin do it deliberately to break the kulaks (with a bit of Ukrainian separatism thrown in) or were these deaths no more than a by-product of an ideological agricultural experiment gone wrong? Most modern famines are. Allowing the experiment to continue rather than changing the ideology is not to commit a holocaust—gross negligence is not murder no matter how gross the negligence. Having a disastrous ideology is not a crime either.

The British are condemned for the Irish Potato Famine which might have the numbers but not, surely, the intent. Elsewhere the British *were* acting with intent, for example forming killing lines to rid Tasmania of aborigines, but that is not even ethnic cleansing, it is a vermin eradication programme. If that is your ideology. But note, the Nazis did not believe Jews were vermin—quite the contrary, they were *competitors*. Nazis understand the difference between propaganda and fact every bit as much as you do.

The intent argument arises in another form with 'Holocaust-deniers' who (quite properly in my opinion) argue (incorrectly in my opinion) that the Jews died from

106

disease, starvation and neglect rather than being marched into gas chambers. Anne Frank did not die from Zyklon-B poisoning but from natural causes—typhus—no matter how unnatural the circumstances. Don't write in.

The third criterion is **justification**. Is killing forty-two thousand people in a Hamburg firestorm justified because the Germans killed five hundred and sixty-eight people in Coventry? Most of us would say it was, this being no more than an eye-for-an-eye added to superior technology, but such arguments can be selective. We do not treat the US killing a hundred thousand in the Tokyo firestorm as morally different from Hamburg despite the Japanese not having bombed a single American city. No doubt they would have if they could have but it remains the case that without eye-for-an-eye justification some nice as pie American said, "We are going to line up a hundred thousand mainly women and children and march them into the ovens."

Were the Nazis *justified* in killing the six million Jews? Yes, they were. It was harsh, I admit, but the fact of the matter is that the Jews were the root cause of most of the ills of Europe and it was simply impractical, in the circumstances of the war, to do anything else. Or at least that is what I would be saying if my schooling had been under the aegis of the Moseley Education Act of 1944 rather than the Butler Education Act of 1944. None of us can help believing what we are taught so lets everyone clamber down from too high a horse.

You can give your own personal felicific calculus a workout on a smaller scale, with this scenario:

> You are a Croat living in a Croat village in Yugoslavia.
> At the other end of the valley is a Serb village. The val-

ley itself is in the nether region between majority Croat territory and majority Serb territory. For five hundred years your two villages have co-existed if not always in amity at least peaceably. For those five hundred years your national government has been neither Serb nor Croat but that is about to change, though whether it is to be Serb or Croat is impossible to discern at this point in time.

You are called to a meeting at the village hall to be addressed by a 'Croat militia commander' (who elected him? you think to yourself). He explains, as if you didn't know, there is a fair possibility that a Croatia and a Serbia is going to come into existence in the very near future and there is a reasonable possibility that your two villages may not be peaceably co-existing in the very near future. "Oh, why is that?" you ask, "we've managed well enough for five hundred years."

"Well, for a start," he answers, "a Serb militia commander is addressing them in their village hall as I speak." So yes, you reluctantly agree, a local unit of the Croat militia to defend yourselves does not seem unreasonable.

"Defence only," you say to general acclaim, "we've got nothing against them as neighbours."

"Fair enough," he continues smoothly, "but you do have a further option. Facts on the ground will dictate where the border gets drawn and a Serb-free valley will likely get you into Croatia. Boundary commissions have enough problems on their plate without worrying how they got there. Will you agree to the militia being used to drive the Serbs out?"

"Not in a million years," you say to general acclaim, "we'll take our chances about where the border falls."

"That's all very well," he points out, "but the Serbs are discussing the exact same things. How confident are you they will come to the same conclusion?"

"Very confident. Serbs are much like Croats. Sure, there will be hotheads arguing for this or that but we've known our local Serbs for five hundred years. Believe me, wiser heads will prevail."

The militia commander sighs. "What you say is all too true but misses the point. Every village in Yugoslavia wants 'defensive measures only' but that is not the view of, as it were, the *national* militias. You will not be defending yourselves against your Serb neighbours but against Serb 'ethnic cleansing units' acting with an eye to where the national borders will eventually be drawn."

"What does that mean in practice?"

"Well, *our* policy is to concentrate on mixed valleys in the doubtful areas in order to create 'facts on the ground', so probably that is the Serb policy as well. As you say, they are remarkably like us."

"I understand all that," you say, "I read the papers, but I say again, what does it mean in practice?"

"It is very simple. Some Serbs will show up one day and kill enough of you to persuade everyone else to pack up and leave."

"Isn't that why we have our defensive militia, to prevent exactly that?"

"No, they will come with overwhelming force—they've got an entire national militia to call on."

"What's the alternative?"

"If you drive your local Serbs out of this valley now, the 'national' Serbs will likely accept the verdict to concentrate on other valleys where there are still Serbs. No guarantees but you will probably be left in peace, and you might well end up living in Croatia."

"What does 'driving out our local Serbs' involve?" you ask.

"I've already told you. We kill sufficient Serbs with our ethnic cleansing units. There's no alternative, they have a defensive militia too and an attachment to the land every bit as strong as yours. What works, works."

"And the alternative?" you enquire pensively.

"For you personally? You can pack up now and go off and live as a refugee. As an early adopter you'll probably get into Sweden. But obviously you will be leaving behind your family to be selectively butchered and/or end up as much less salubrious refugees."

"Well, I'm sorry, I'm just not going to do it. My moral compass forbids it."

"Oh, you don't have to *do* anything. You don't even have to approve."

Yugoslavia did not deliver a holocaust—even Srebrenica fell short—but the world is still delivering up holocausts. How are we managing with these? Here's a two-parter for you:

> Question 1: There was a holocaust in central Europe in the nineteen-forties. Was this a case of Germans killing Jews or was it Jews killing Germans?

> Question 2: There was a holocaust in central Africa in the nineteen-nineties. Was this a case of Hutus killing Tutsis or was it Tutsis killing Hutus?

Our hesitancy may not necessarily be racist because we also categorise holocaust-scale events on another basis, the **generative agent**. 'Popular genocides', however much they may be *inspired* by governments, are not the real thing.

110

Just after the war a million people were killed during the partition of India but, however lamented, this is not considered holocaustal because it was 'popular'. The generative agents were neither the British authorities (though their actions were lamentable) nor the Muslim and Hindu authorities (though their actions were lamentable) but 'the people'. People do what people do.

There was also the undoubted boon that the ethnic cleansing produced permanent and stable borders. It is instructive to list the causes of the various Indo-Pakistan wars. None of them was because "You killed half a million of our Muslims/Hindus/Sikhs." By a chilling irony it was because they didn't. India was undoubtedly foolish to insist that Kashmir is a Hindu state despite having a majority Muslim population but it was doubly foolish not to eliminate the Muslim population. Pakistan was foolish differently over Bangladesh.

But even bona fide 'governmental holocausts' may not be treated even-handedly. The peerless Robert Fisk, when reporting on a controversy about the 1915 Turkish genocide of the Armenians, had a long wrangle with his sub-editors as to why this holocaust got a small aitch and only the Jewish Holocaust got a capital. *The Independent* duly changed its house style to give equal treatment to Holocausts but the sub-editors were correct: until something better comes along (journalistically speaking) the Jewish Holocaust is the only one that really counts.

For my part I do not give a fig about the killing of the Jews—it's a historical event, before my time—and though it has taken me some while to achieve such anthropological equanimity, I recommend you do the same. Not to alleviate pain or guilt, that's a bonus, but because these are real issues that need real thought and real thought requires real detachment. You can't do cancer research if, every time you see a cancer cell down the microscope, you start jumping up and down shouting, "You killed my granny." But a word of warning: you won't be thanked. You will be thoroughly excoriated. I dunno, the world we live in.

*   *   *

25   Napoleon and Hitler

The British often bracket Napoleon and Hitler together as ogres though the French are infuriated by any such comparison. The Germans are more nuanced. What cannot be denied is that, given they are the only two individuals ever to subjugate (nearly) the whole of Europe, they might reward comparison in purely military terms.

We can begin with what caused their end. Invading Russia. That they *were* invasions is critical. France had had no difficulty beating the Russians 1793-1807, Germany equally so 1914-17, but that was when it was Russia doing the invading. Lenin's famous summing up of how the world works—*who whom?*—is often decisive in Great Power conflict because of the morale factor (not the moral factor, which I leave to others). Citizens of Great Powers quite like going to war, it is what being a citizen of a Great Power is all about, but they get restive if the war lasts too long. Then 'who started it?' becomes all too relevant, violation being a better recruiting sergeant than adventurism.

One of the differences between Korea and Vietnam was that the Americans were responding to an invasion in Korea but in Vietnam they were merely projecting their dominant power. Again, with the First Gulf War they were responding to an invasion; the Second Gulf War was just more system management by the dominant power. It is always fun becoming the dominant power, it is always hell being the dominant power. One feels for China.

Though both Napoleon and Hitler 'started it' when they invaded Russia, they were acting quite reasonably in terms of controlling the prevailing Great Power System. As it was the *same* system, even if a century apart, it is not surprising they were trying to control the same situation:

1. Both had virtually complete control of the continent of Europe
2. Both were at war with Britain, a Great Power that could not threaten them militarily but could not be dealt with militarily either
3. Both faced Russia, a Great Power that might threaten them militarily but could be dealt with militarily
4. Both were formally allied with Russia.

This meant Russia and Britain were notionally opposed but neither Napoleon nor Hitler could allow the situation to persist indefinitely because Britain would continue to fight so long as Russia was a potential ally in the east, and Russia would continue to act quasi-independently so long as Britain was a complication in the west. Napoleon and Hitler both assumed they would win against Russia, and win easily because

1. Each had been enjoying a remarkable run of military successes
2. Russia had a no less spectacular record of recent military failures
3. As dominant powers they could both assemble Grande Armées for their invasions, composed of a core of their own troops plus contributions from half-a-dozen other European countries
4. Both were able to start from the same favourable vantage point, deep inside Poland.

So why did both invasions go so disastrously wrong? The most commonly cited answer is 'the vast distances of the Russian interior' but they are vast for Russia too. Nor are they particularly vast. The distance from the Polish frontier to Moscow is comparable to the distance from the south coast of England to Inverness and it is unlikely, should historians have been called upon to explain the epic failures of the 1805 and 1940 invasions of Britain, that 'the vast distances of the British interior' would be cited as the decisive factor.

The argument has always to be buttressed by its evil twin, 'General Winter', but this is equally doubtful. The French had already been badly mauled at Borodino in the summer and it was Russian counterattacks that did for them during the winter retreat, though they don't like to admit it. The Germans actually waited for winter before launching their attack on Moscow because frozen ground suited their style of warfare better than the cloying mud of the autumn *rasputitsa*.

Historians are also adamant about how these malign stars got lined up: it was all down to failings in the respective generalship of Napoleon and Hitler. This is convenient because the real reason—the Russians were just plain better—is an uncomfortable truth. The Bear lurking in his primeval forest is one of those world bogeymen that always have to be exorcised along with the Yellow Peril, the Grand Turk, assorted sun kings, militant Catholicism, militant Marxism, militant Islam, militant Americanism. These *Weltangshauung* forebodings were very much to the fore when it came to both Napoleon and Hitler. Napoleonic France was at the furthest left of the contemporary political spectrum, Tsarist Russia equally far out on the right; ditto but reversed second time round, now it was Hitler representing the far right, Stalin the extreme left. What does this tell us about extremist politics in global affairs? They are harbingers of the future? The failed lessons of the past? It takes one to beat one?

Neither Napoleon nor Hitler allowed ideology to drive their foreign policies. Egoism did that, which meant the 'personal' affected their decision-making more than is usual for Great Powers. Napoleon felt personally betrayed by Tsar Alexander after their love-in at Tilsit; Hitler felt personally affronted when, after he thought he had so cleverly boxed the Soviets in with the Molotov-Ribbentrop Pact, Stalin effortlessly outmanoeuvred him for the next year and a half. Never mind national self-interest, these two people must be punished. Personally.

This affected the *conduct* of the campaigns too. Napoleon 'knew his man' and calculated he could force Alexander to the negotiating table and back under his spell by occupying Moscow. Surely the Little Father would not countenance such a blow to the heart of Mother Russia? Yes, he could. Hitler was so determined to take the eponymous city of Stalingrad the 1942 campaign was skewed to that end. That would force the brute to make peace. Stalin did not oblige. Projective identification is always a problem for egoists. You should read the therapy notes for Donald Trump and Kim Jung-un.

In *system* terms, 1812 and 1941 were the right wars fought in the wrong way. Both Napoleon and Hitler were moulded by the army so it occurred to neither man there is another way of controlling Europe. *By sea.* They knew they could never beat the British in a fleet action but forgot the lesson taught by that other serial expansionist, Alexander the Great: the ocean can be conquered from the land.

Nobody ever gives serious thought about why Napoleon headed for Moscow rather than the actual Russian capital, St Petersburg, but Napoleon should have given it some serious thought. The *system* reason for Napoleon's invasion of Russia was Tsar Alexander's flouting of the Berlin Decrees by trading with the British, which was not damaging in itself but had the effect of allowing the other Baltic states to tacitly evade their obligations as well. And so on through the system. Since all Europe wanted to trade with Britain, it could only get worse. A *systems* Napoleon, as opposed to a Mad Dog Napoleon, would have treated this as just one more problem facing a dominant power and solved it by making the Baltic a French *lac*. This did not require beating the British at sea because the Baltic was already very nearly a Napoleonic lac

1. Prussia was a client
2. Sweden and Finland were governed by one of his marshals
3. Denmark was fed up with British bombardments
4. Only Russia was a problem.

Occupy St Petersburg and the problem goes away. Russia would not have gone away but then, as any sensible Great Power knows, Russia never goes away, it can only be dealt with on a case by case basis. Napoleon found this out for himself when, after reducing Russia to a rump and scattering her armies, the rump and the armies were soon back in the lists.

Hitler lacked the same sense of perspective. Even if *Barbarossa* had been successful, it is doubtful Russia would have 'gone away'. It is often forgotten that the German war aim was to occupy Russia up to the Volga and leave a Russian rump state in being on the other side, and this was largely achieved at Stalingrad. It availed Germany nothing. The Russia Hitler was facing in the autumn of 1942 was the same rump state created by Brest Litovsk in 1918, the same rump state the Mongols supposed they had left prostrate, the same rump state facing NATO today after the 1991 demise of the Soviet Union. It makes not the slightest difference, Russia is Russia wherever it hangs its hat.

What should Hitler have done to solve his Russian problem? Stalin was upsetting Hitler's Continental System as much as Tsar Alexander was Napoleon's so *something* had to be done. If only he would postpone his Lebensraum obsessions for a year or two Hitler might have profited from noting how, ironically, Napoleon's nephew reined Russia in with his Crimean War of 1853-6. There is a lot to be said for soft underbellies.

The Mediterranean had been a British preserve since before there was a Britain (Rooke took Gibraltar in 1704, Britain started out in 1707). There had been no significant German presence in the Mediterranean, not even a Habsburg German presence, for the whole period from 1704 until 1941, by which date a series of fortuitous developments had changed the position dramatically. A tour round the Mediterranean shows the extent of German control:

1. Italy was a formal German ally
2. France was a German client following her defeat and part-occupation
3. Spain was officially neutral but in practice a German co-belligerent
4. North Africa was either Spanish or French or Italian
5. Lebanon and Syria were French
6. Turkey was pro-British but obliged to follow pro-German policies
7. The Balkans were occupied by Axis troops
8. Only Egypt and Palestine were in British hands.

The Mediterranean had become as pro-German in 1941 as the Baltic had been pro-French in 1812. The entire littoral was in friendly hands apart from one corner, Alexandria corresponding to St Petersburg and, as luck would have it, just as Napoleon had forces in Poland threatening St Petersburg, so Hitler had the Afrika Korps threatening Alexandria.

All Hitler had to do was ignore the siren calls of dealing with Russia and deal with Britain instead. The British would certainly have been dealt with because the three German divisions of the Afrika Korps and a single Luftflotte had all but routed them so calling on two hundred divisions and the whole Luft*waffe* would presumably have got the job done. The Germans would have rapidly come to control Egypt, Palestine, Iraq and Iran; Turkey would be even more a German protectorate than it already was; without Alexandria, Malta is untenable and Gibraltar irrelevant. The Royal Navy, and with it the British, would have been banished to the Atlantic and Indian Oceans. For Germany there would now be no southern front at all, only further territories to exploit.

Would any of this have made a decisive difference to the outcome of the Second World War? Not directly as Britain would have carried on fighting even after losing the Middle East—if we are to believe the cabinet papers—and Russia would still have to be dealt with. One of the abiding sins of Hitlerian grand strategy was the non-concentration of force at the decisive point, so is this not more of the same? Quite the reverse. By *not* eliminating the British in Egypt, Hitler was obliged to pour more and more resources into the Mediterranean ulcer. More Axis troops surrendered at Tunis than at Stalingrad.

Not that the Battle of Stalingrad would have happened in the first place since, with ample oil supplies from the Middle East, Hitler would hardly have launched his quixotic advance towards the Caucasus oilfields. Concentration of force is now Stalin's problem: with a handful of German troops on the other side of the Caucasus, it would be the Russians expending large forces defending *their* oil.

Would a 1942 or a 1943 Barbarossa have turned out differently from a 1941 Barbarossa? Probably not. The Russians would have found a way to win somehow. They did, after all, win in the end with plenty to spare. Even so a *German* Palestine in 1941 could have had one lasting effect: the Wannsee Conference of 1942 would surely have had a different agenda. It is often assumed Hitler was contemptuous of Jews but this is not so. He feared them. In Europe. But nothing beats having six million Zionists as your sheriff in the Middle East.

*   *   *

26 Gentlemen and Players

Until the 1960's one of the highlights of the English summer was a cricket match between the Gentlemen (amateurs) and the Players (professionals). This was not as one-sided as might be expected because the Gentlemen were paid more than the Players. They were upper class types who got 'emoluments' whereas the Players were more your wage labourers. Strangely enough everybody believed it really was amateurs against professionals. The Gentlemen had somehow wandered in from their country houses for a spot of cricket with the chaps from the village, but on a national scale. Naturally it was played at Lords, the 'home of cricket'. Technically *Lord's*—it is named for its builder, Thomas Lord, not the British class system—except it was paid for by my lords Winchelsea and Richmond.

The perceived virtues of amateurism were so cherished by the British they applied the principle to war. Indeed war itself was seen as a sort of regular sporting fixture, the British army on tour against whichever bunch of indigenes needing incorporation into the Empire that year, which for the British was pretty much every year. This sporting leit-motif reached its apogee in 1940 with the newspaper plac-ard announcing the Fall of France as "We're in the Final now!" This jollification of war might be mocked by our more cynical selves but it has one overarching benefit: amateurs playing at war excuses military defeats at the hands of those who make a career of it.

Perhaps the best remembered example of the syndrome is the tweedy bespectacled Barnes Wallis in the *Dam Busters* film trying to perfect the bouncing bomb by firing marbles across a rain barrel in his back garden. No doubt this was accurate enough but the film forgot to mention Barnes Wallis was a chief designer at Vickers, Britain's largest armaments manufacturer. He was the ultimate professional. This meant the next scene, a nervous Wallis hanging around the vestibule of the Air Ministry, was filmed in the wrong vestibule. It was more a case of "Please, could you send a message up to Mr Wallis and ask him if he wouldn't mind awfully designing some better bombs for our main bomber type, the Wellington. He'll know the specifications, he designed that one as well."

We like the *idea* of Young Lochinvar versus Colonel Blimp but wars are best left in the hands of Colonel Blimp. Novel weapons are always necessary, they are always being proposed, they always turn out to be impractical. Or nearly so. They have to be winnowed by the people who are going to use them and long experience is that they are mostly impractical. The bouncing bomb was never used again.

The maverick inventor may be a British trope but this does not make it untrue. The British are historically the world champions of inventiveness and inventions are characteristically the brainchilds of amateurs. However, when it comes to war, time is of the essence so it is better to seek out the amateurs rather than leave them in their garden sheds. (American-British: garages.)

Radar always gets brandished as a British invention and the usual owlish figure in plus-fours, Robert Watson-Watt, is given the credit. Up to a point, Lord Rank. Watson-Watt had been asked to do it by the government in the early thirties and the Germans were not only doing it as well, they were doing it better. For example, when the war started not a single British warship had radar and the admirals were staggered to find the *Graf Spee* festooned with some very advanced arrays. It says something about the professionalism of naval intelligence they found this out from American press photos taken of the *Graf Spee* in Montevideo harbour.

The British did come up with one bright radar idea. They gave all their radar technology free, gratis and for nothing to the neutral Americans. They did ask for the Norden bombsight in exchange but the Americans told them to get lost. Still, it was just in time for the Americans to install an experimental radar set at Pearl Harbour and launch a thousand conspiracy theories about how they knew the Japs were coming all right but Roosevelt wanted them to sink enough ships to persuade an enraged nation to go to war with Germany. Something like that, but anyway when the enraged Yanks *were* finally aboard, their military-industrial complex could be welded to British ingenuity and Allied radar was taken to vistas quite beyond the increasingly befuddled Germans. That bit is true.

We also invented the jet engine, didn't we? Owlish plus-foured Frank Whittle and all that? Sort of. Hans von Ohain had come up with much the same idea in Germany and they were better on the technical side so when the Luftwaffe were deploying the phenomenal Messerschmitt Me-262 the RAF were still tinkering with the phenomenally lacklustre Gloster Meteor. British jets did come into their own during the *Korean* War because the government had given all their jet technology free, gratis and for nothing to the Russians as a thank-you for winning the war and maybe helping out with the peace. Once British ingenuity had been welded to the Soviet military-industrial complex,

MiG-15's could start shooting American Shooting Stars out of the sky. Serves them right for that Norden business.

Not to mention the atom bomb, another joint wartime venture the Americans later refused to share with the British. The Americans did give the Bomb free, gratis and for nothing to the Russians because Russian spies were better than British spies at getting hold of American atom secrets. Or to be more accurate, British atom spies—Nunn May, Klaus Fuchs, Bruno Pontecorvo and the ones we don't know about—were Russian atom spies. On the other hand the British did get the Bomb as suspiciously early as the Russians so there may be more to this story than they are letting on. Whoever 'they' are.

Inventions often seemed to be lauded in inverse proportion to their usefulness, D-Day being an especially fertile source for such legends. The British invented and then built at incredible expense artificial harbours that could be towed across the Channel, the *Mulberries*. One for our sector, one for the American sector. Soon after installation the American Mulberry was badly damaged in a storm and they decided to abandon it because, as they pointed out to the British, they could bring stuff directly over the beaches just as easily using roll-on/roll-off ferries.

The British answered this slight with PLUTO, Pipeline Under the Ocean, which could bring fuel over in vast quantities without need of either Mulberries or Ro-Ro's. And by Jove it did, after the war, pumping petrol to the French while they were getting their bombed refineries back on stream. *During* the war teething problems with PLUTO meant all the oil had to go over by ship after all.

Then there were 'the funnies', specially prepared tanks for assaulting the hugely costly and fiendishly constructed

German Atlantic Wall. How useful were they? We will never know because the Poles and Ukrainians defending the redoubts on behalf of the Germans did not think being entombed in concrete part of their new citizenship duties and surrendered with such promptitude the Atlantic Wall held up the British for all of half an hour.

Today our favourite wartime amateurs are the denizens of Bletchley Park—varsity types, chess-playing poets, Sloane Rangers of varying genders—confounding those extremely professional Germans. What's the real story? When a country switches from peace to war there is an unavoidable dislocation of the economy as certain sectors expand and others are curtailed. One of the occupations not required are university lecturers whose charges are either at war or should be. One sector that *is* required and in great numbers is that of cryptographer/cryptanalyst (the distinction is secret). Where does a professional war machine go to find such people? Is it a) Oxbridge to recruit mathematicians or is it b) the Rhondda Valley to recruit coal miners?

The Intelligence War as a whole is a good place for applying the amateurism-is-best principle because professional intelligence services are institutionally incompetent by virtue of their secretiveness. Who's to know? At the outbreak of war, the British Secret Service was feared and respected throughout the world which was strange because it amounted to little more than Passport Control Officers (the standard cover for MI6 personnel in British embassies) sending in kaffeeklatsch gossip and newspaper clippings. To be fair, they did have a network of secret agents in Europe at the start of the war but these were rounded up by the Germans after two of MI6's most senior people managed to get themselves captured on the Dutch/German border and promptly told everything they knew. Without, to be fair, much coercion according to German records inspected after the war.

With the agents gone and the passport offices closed, MI6 was reduced to minor operations in neutral capitals. However MI6 emerged from the war with its reputation enhanced because what it is really good at is Whitehall politicking. It carefully arranged to be *ex officio* in charge of Bletchley Park—to which otherwise it had no practical connection—and C (or M as we have learned to call her) would daily plonk juicy Bletchley morsels on Churchill's desk. Since everybody else, for security reasons, had to be told this cascade of information about German strengths and intentions was being derived not from code-breaking but from 'secret agents', everybody just loved MI6 and their secret agents. For security reasons this policy had to be continued after the war so everybody continued to love MI6 and its secret agents after the war. How long would these security considerations have to stay in place before the true story could be told? Hard to say, it's a question best left to the professionals at MI6.

Meanwhile there was a *consciously* amateur spy outfit being put together next door. The Ministry of Economic Warfare was one of Churchill's pets but its main role—predicting when Germany would run out of essentials and how to hasten that day—was hamstrung by the fact that it was always predicting the Germans were running out of everything and they never did. The services took no notice of these forecasts when framing their own plans but as Churchill retained faith in his MEW, they often had to hide this by creative memo writing. "Yes, Prime Minister, there certainly are oil refineries in Hamburg."

As the new ministry did not have anything very useful to do, it was put in charge of the even newer Special Operations Executive whose remit was to 'set Europe ablaze' using any method not requiring regular forces. Nothing to do with economic warfare but it kept them out of the service departments' hair. Not out of MI6's hair since the professional spies did not much care for SOE people blowing things up when their own people were trying to avoid attention.

Whether the SOE was value for money during the war is arguable but the blowback *after* the war, when the techniques pioneered by the SOE were used against them, cost the British an arm and a leg. Whether terrorists are amateurs or professionals can also be argued but whether terrorism *per se* is a good thing or a bad thing is seldom argued. If they are ours (SOE, the French Resistance, Yugoslav partisans, Norwegian saboteurs) they are good, if not they are bad, though occasionally, like the Jewish Irgun, they are good, then bad, then the government.

Britain took a further step by applying the amateur principle to the professional army. As a maritime power Britain has no peacetime conscription so when a big war does come along her armies are invariably amateurs with a crust of professionals. Crusty professionals because, without conscription, the officers and NCO's are also unused to handling massed soldiery. It is not an ideal combination, the upshot being the British (and the Americans who are in the same boat) are never brilliant when it comes to large armies. Nobody likes admitting their soldiers aren't a patch on *their* soldiers so the British, and later the Americans, started casting around for soldiers who were a patch and came up with the concept of the 'private army'.

These were, one might say, institutionalised amateurs, self-contained formations inspired by and largely composed of people not comfortably contained within the regular ranks but nonetheless 'ardent spirits'. Each outfit was given an evocative—or a mysterious—name like the Commandos, the Rangers, SAS, SBS, OSS, the Long Range Desert Group, the Airborne, the Chindits, Merrill's Marauders, Special Forces and so forth. And so forth and so forth because whatever their limitations fighting the enemy they were just the job for generating cheerful news stories at home.

They could even be useful strategically. Global war means global arguments so when, say, Churchill and Roosevelt are at Quebec in 1943 and Churchill wants a Burma campaign and all the Burma campaigns have so far been resounding failures, *and* the Americans are disinclined to help out with a new one, he can ask General Wingate to attend the conference and explain in person to Roosevelt how the Chindits are going to change all that. Roosevelt can then nod sagely and assure Churchill that his own Merrill's Marauders will back them to the hilt. Honour is satisfied, concord reigns, communiqués issued. The regular generals, Auchinleck and Stillwell, can then get on fighting the Japanese. And one another. And Churchill and Roosevelt.

How effective were these private armies when it came to fighting the enemy? Actually, very effective. If you collect the most ardent spirits and put them into specialised units you can do some real damage. It means fewer ardent spirits in the regular ranks which is regrettable because all armies rely on ardent spirits to persuade less ardent spirits to go over the top. Doubtless it is a coincidence that British

and American armies seldom went over the top to any
great effect during the Second World War.

*   *   *

27 Behind the Wire

After the war the British became enamoured with prisoner
of war books. They couldn't get enough of them. Films too,
The Great Escape was shown every Christmas along with
the Queen and the Two Ronnies.

We are all familiar with the phrase 'Name, rank and
number' because military personnel are instructed to tell
their captors only their name (so the Red Cross can tell
their relatives), rank (officers get better treatment) and
service number (armies run on them). They may receive
condign punishment from their own side if they say more.
We like to believe our boys were like dad and kept mum
but in reality they blabbed to high heaven. I cannot say this
for sure—it is not something that gets much written
about—but it is true of every other army.

It is to mutual advantage that enemy soldiers surrender
rather than fight to the last man so 'rules of war' about
prisoners have evolved over the centuries. Basically, once
through 'processing' (the blabbing part) prisoners are to
be allowed to sit out the war in relative safety. 'Relative'
meaning 'relative to dying in battle'. A low hurdle admit-
tedly but there is another safeguard: the knowledge that
what you are doing to theirs they can do to yours, though
this did not apply when fighting countries like the Soviet
Union or Japan who disapproved of their soldiers surrendering in the first place. All the combatants were in theory
signed up to formal conventions about the treatment of
prisoners but since the warring nations knew they would
either win or be punished for much graver offences if they
lost, these were *variously* applied.

For instance, prisoners could not be forced to work but 'volunteers' might do non-war work—repairing bombed out cities, working on farms, that sort of thing—but this is a tricky distinction in conditions of total war. Not only for the captors, POWs might be shot by their own side for aiding and abetting the enemy if they got it wrong. This was variously applied. The most successful British escape of the war was a working party repairing the strategically vital Slovenian railways and they were given an admiring documentary on Channel 4, not the firing squad.

According to the British, it is an officer's *duty* to escape. As a corollary his captors, also officers, are expected to go along with the practice in a good sport sort of way, ('twenty-eight days in the cooler'). But this too can be variously applied. Civilian escapes can be discouraged by tacking on another couple of years to the original sentence, a couple of years cannot be tacked on to a war. When over-all numbers rule out an elaborate infrastructure of prison buildings, preventing escapes is all that is possible and it becomes something of a test for both sides. This 'war be-hind the wire' is presumably what makes the POW genre so compelling. Not to Hitler who was unamused not so much by British officers doing their duty as by the massive manhunts and alarums triggered by them doing so. He proposed various exemplary punishments to stop them trying but the British announced that whatever he did to recaptured British escapees, they would do to *all* German prisoners and it was soon back to twenty-eight days in the cooler. Heart of gold that Hitler.

Until the Great Escape when he had fifty of the recap-tured prisoners shot. A war crime? Not necessarily. There are two conflicting principles here. The first is that indeed prisoners of war are entitled to escape if they can and are

131

not to be unduly punished for attempting to do so. This was scrupulously adhered to by the Germans as far as British prisoners were concerned and vice versa. However, there is another 'usage of war' which is that enemy combatants found in civilian clothes may be shot, and both Germans and British scrupulously adhered to that one as well. What happens when the two principles collide? If you organise a mass escape of two hundred prisoners of war and if you state, as the organiser of the Great Escape did, that your aim is not primarily to get back to Blighty but to tie up as many German military resources as possible in the mass searches that will inevitably ensue, are you an escaping POW or are you a hostile combatant in civilian clothes?

I'd let Hitler off on this one. The only war crime associated with the Great Escape was the judicial murder, on the orders of the post-war British government, of German individuals who had personally executed the escapees. They were hanged despite the fact they had no option when shooting the recaptured prisoners other than refusing and being shot themselves. The Nuremberg Trials established that 'following orders' is not a defence to war crimes. Sometimes it isn't, sometimes it is.

Hitler cannot be so easily acquitted over the 3.3 million Russian POWs who died, more than half of all Red Army soldiers captured. The sheer number puts us in holocaust territory and while evidence of deliberation is unclear, it was certainly uncaring neglect on a holocaustal scale. A monstrous crime but also a curious one. Germany was short of manpower throughout the war, making Russian prisoners valuable not only as labourers but as actual soldiers fighting on the German side in the Vlasov Army and other *Ost* formations. So the deaths of these 3.3 million Russians appears to be not only a crime but a blunder.

Russian *survivors* of German ill-treatment did not get a home town parade once back in the motherland, unless their home was a gulag, but it was no better for captured *German* soldiers. Eastern Front figures are always flexible but if we take the reasonably well-documented Battle of Stalingrad as a guide, of the quarter-million German soldiers who fought there, upwards of 150,000 died during the battle and a hundred thousand were taken prisoner. Out of the hundred thousand, about five thousand eventually got back to *their* motherland. Entering the Battle of Stalingrad had a survival rate much the same as entering Auschwitz. Possibly some rough justice there.

The Anglo-Americans operated on a smaller scale, had better logistics and superior societal values. At the societal level. On the battlefield it could be different. The problem facing their soldiers is one facing all soldiers: if you capture one of the enemy that means one less for their side but taking the prisoner back typically requires two of yours to escort him. One for two. Soldiers do not ordinarily favour actions that lessen their own chances so it is by no means unknown for prisoners to be quietly shot. Plus, people enjoy killing people who have just been killing their closest companions. Plus, people enjoy killing people. It does have to be done quietly though because all armies have a theoretical prohibition against killing prisoners out of hand (to encourage surrender). I cannot say whether the British killed their prisoners, they are good at covering these things up, but Americans suffer from the First Amendment so I can say that G.I.'s shot prisoners out of hand on quite a generous scale.

As I write, some of the trickier aspects of the dilemma are playing out nightly on the news. Three hundred and fifty prisoners have just been liberated from Ghazni Jail in Central Afghanistan during a Taliban raid. Are you allowed to shoot the prisoners as soon as it is clear they will be freed? No. Are you allowed to shoot them as they escape? Sort of, in a collateral sort of way. Are you allowed to shoot them after they have joined their Taliban comrades in the hills? Yes. So at what point does the situation change? Is there a bloke in a UN helmet with a flag saying, "Begin shooting ... now!"

*   *   *

28   Going Down With The Ship

We are surprised, shocked, to read about Japanese battle-field statistics in the Second World War. A typical sequence might be

1. three thousand Japanese soldiers form a garrison on a Pacific island
2. the Americans arrive in overwhelming force
3. some days/weeks later the Americans capture the island
4. the Americans have five hundred casualties, of which a hundred are fatal
5. the Japanese have three thousand casualties, of which all are fatal
6. four survivors are later found hiding in a cave who always turn out to be Koreans.

This idea of fighting literally to the last man is alien to our western sensibilities. We might admire Japanese sold-iers' loyalty and bravery but we would not wish to live in a society that demanded it. Unless we are British. Our nat-ional icon, the Royal Navy, operated a similar doctrine in the Second World War. Sailors were not permitted to sur-render but must fight on until their ship was sunk.

The case of HMS *Rawalpindi* is instructive. Before the war the Rawalpindi had been a P & O cruise liner but in 1939 she was given some obsolescent guns and sent off to patrol the North Atlantic with a watching brief for disguis-ed German merchant vessels similarly armed. What she actually encountered were the German battleships *Scharn-horst* and *Gneisenau*. Rawalpindi reported their course and position to the Admiralty and was twice invited to surrender by the Germans. Instead Rawalpindi took on the battleships, to be rapidly sunk with the loss of two hundred and forty from her crew of three hundred. Her captain was given a minor posthumous award for doing his duty but there was nothing for anybody else because nobody else had demonstrated any personal bravery above and beyond following orders. In fact anyone who objected to the prospect of imminent and rather pointless death would have been awarded a court martial.

Today we might tut-tut at such a top-loaded honours system but as far as the Rawalpindi, her captain and her crew are concerned we would (at worst) shrug and (at best) be proud. It is what the Royal Navy does. It is what the Royal Navy is *for*. It would not stop us accusing Japanese soldiers of inbred fatalism, blind obedience, savage fanaticism, Emperor worship and any other negative stereotype that might spring to our tiny Chinese minds.

*   *   *

29 Senior Service

The Royal Navy is one of those institutions that have gone from world-beaters to basket cases in a single generation.

The Navy's record in the First World War had been rather good—especially Jellicoe's masterly conduct of the Battle of Jutland—and by 1919, after the German fleet had scuttled itself at Scapa Flow, it had uncontested world supremacy. Its nearest rival was the US Navy, and while there were definite undercurrents that one day this situation might have to be addressed, that day did not arrive during the Second World War when the two navies elected to fight in separate hemispheres.

The one blemish on the Royal Navy's First War escutcheon had been its inability to deal with German submarines. The U-boats sank so many merchant ships in 1917 they came close to costing Britain the war. The problem was solved by the politicians insisting, largely against the admirals' objections, that convoys be instituted. The convoys' naval escorts sank few German submarines but because the merchant ships were now concentrated it was as difficult finding a convoy as it was encountering a single ship, so the submarines no longer sank many ships. One other factor helped: wireless was in its infancy so convoys did not have their whereabouts constantly relayed to eavesdropping Germans as was the case in the Second War when the combined incompetence of GCHQ (as it then wasn't) and the Admiralty meant the Germans were reading convoy codes in real time.

But this was all to come. In the interwar years, with Germany having no significant battle fleet, it was self-evident that the Royal Navy's number one task in any future naval war with Germany would be convoy protection. Alas! The one thing the navy disdains more than the army is the merchant navy. For twenty years nobody at the Admiralty paid much attention to convoy tactics, hardly any escort ships were built and merchant protection did not figure in the annual exercises except as a way of drawing in a lot of big ships banging away at one another.

Whenever anybody pointed out the convoy lacuna, the admirals had a one-word answer, 'ASDIC'. Sonar, as it is now called, was a method of detecting submarines underwater and the navy decided that therefore submarines were no longer a problem. This would have been sound thinking if submarines had in fact been submarines but at this stage of their development they were more 'submersible torpedo boats', deployed on the surface, firing their torpedoes and deck guns exactly as a destroyer would. ASDIC did not detect submarines on the surface. When the war started in 1939 all that saved Britain from an immediate 1917-style debâcle was that German admirals were also fans of banging away with big ships and had spent *their* interwar years building battleships and cruisers, not submarines.

Once this policy was corrected (by Hitler) and once the Kriegsmarine had acquired Atlantic bases after the fall of France, effectively doubling the number of operational U-boats, the havoc could begin. The Royal Navy could not help but notice yet another war was in danger of being lost on its watch and dug out the manuals that had worked the oracle before. Convoys were instituted and escort vessels started coming down the slipways in belated numbers. As the naval staff had not studied the problem and proper shipyards were needed for proper ships, they seized on the

cheap and cheerful, build-anywhere, 'Flower-class' corvette as their standard convoy escort. The design was
based on a deep sea whaler and worked well with whales
but was less effective against submarines that were often
faster than they were. Always a handicap in a sub-chaser.

It turned out escorts were not the answer anyway. If
there were few escorts, the submarines could easily evade
them—U-boats had such a low silhouette they could sail
straight through a convoy at night unnoticed. If the escorts
were many, the submarines formed wolf packs and overwhelmed them. For three and a half years such vast ton-
nages of shipping were lost that Britain's survival seemed
largely down to Hitler's penchant for occupying countries
like Norway and Greece, with some of the largest merchant fleets in the world and now no home ports to call their
own. Even these windfall ships would run out eventually
but, long before that point might be reached, Britain would
have prodigious quantities of a weapon that solved the
submarine problem at a stroke. This is the story of how
they didn't get to use it.

The *Type VII,* the standard German Atlantic submarine
throughout the war, was excellent on the surface and could
run rings round a convoy, both to reach the ideal firing
position and to evade the escorts, but it had a limited
performance *under* water. It could scarcely keep up with a
convoy when submerged. All the British had to do, it
seemed, was to make German submarines dive for any
length of time and the convoy would escape. How to do
this, wondered the British admirals, build more escorts to
keep them down? That did not work because U-boats could
shadow convoys out of range of the escorts by day, then
skip past them at night.

All this changes dramatically when there is a plane above the convoy. A plane will see a submarine at virtually the same moment the submarine sees the plane so a U-boat captain has a choice: stay on the surface and engage the plane or crash dive. If fight is preferred to flight the odds were very much on the side of the submarine—the plane would either miss or be shot down. That is not the relevant equation. A U-boat is worth many times the value of a plane, so the submarine would have to win five, ten, fifty such engagements to show a profit. Nor need the plane attack, it need not be armed, because it can call up a convoy escort and a surfaced submarine stands much less of a chance even against a corvette.

So it was standard operating procedure to crash dive on sighting a plane. A Type VII will disappear in less than a minute meaning no attack from the plane, no attack from an escort. So far so good. However, the U-boat cannot know how long the plane will be around, nor whether an alerted escort will arrive (with ASDIC), so it is obliged to take radical evasive measures to get as far away from the place of sighting as possible. At the same time the convoy will be making course changes on its own account. Given U-boat speeds above or below the surface, it is fair odds the submarine will not regain contact with the convoy.

The plane overhead does not have to be there continuously, or even most of the time. Any plane at any time during the daylight hours will have this general effect on shadowing submarines, so a single patrol once a day may be all that is necessary. As there were seldom more than half a dozen convoys in the North Atlantic at any one time, the task facing the British Admiralty seemed straightforward enough: arrange for half a dozen convoys to have regular visits from half a dozen aircraft. There was no problem with the technology, a British military plane had made the first Atlantic crossing in 1919 and there had been twenty years of non-stop development in every branch of aviation since. Except one.

During those twenty years it was the air force the navy was not getting along with, the basis of the antagonism being the 1918 decision to place all aviation under the newly founded RAF. What had seemed a tidy administrative arrangement at the time meant the navy's Fleet Air Arm was henceforth destined to be an integral part of the RAF. As airplanes were henceforth destined to be the cutting edge of naval warfare this was a bit like putting admirals in charge of armoured divisions. Could have happened! It was the navy that had invented the tank, a Churchillian brainwave after sailors had fought as infantry outside Antwerp in 1914. It does happen in America where the US Navy, aka the Marine Corps, fights the US Army on all fronts and that necessitates equipping the marines with tanks.

The British are more restrained in matters of divided command so the sailors, after 1918, had to go cap in hand to the RAF for their aviation requirements. The air marshals, though anxious to show willing in this unexpected addition to their portfolio, had a strict list of priorities: strategic bombing came first, shooting down other people's strategic bombers came a poor second, helping out the navy came around seventeenth. After years of incessant Whitehall warfare, the navy finally got its aircraft back in 1938 but if they thought the battle won they had vastly underestimated their enemy. "All right then," said the air marshals, "any plane taking off from a ship is yours, any plane taking off from land is ours." "That makes no sense," spluttered the admirals, "we are trained to find and sink ships, you are not, what difference does it make whether the plane takes off from a ship or from land?" "Take it or leave it."

They had to take it. All long-range anti-submarine planes had to take off from land, all short-range patrols would take off from land anyway, so the navy was obliged to regard the entire Air Battle of the Atlantic as being literally none of its business. The RAF did not believe swanning around the Atlantic any of its business either so it was the German submarines and the German long-range anti-shipping aircraft that did the swanning.

'Long range' meant heavy four-engined aircraft and these had two military applications at the time: bombing Germany and dealing with submarines far out to sea. It followed that every four-engined plane coming out of a British factory could do one but only at the expense of the other. Fortunately the one can be readily converted to the other because without a bombload there was masses of room for extra fuel, spare crews, even a depth charge or two, and the priority was stark enough. The bombing of Germany was proving ineffectual, the submarine menace was losing Britain the war.

If the Navy and the RAF had been fighting their corners in the normal way—in Cabinet committee, at the Joint Chiefs, bearding the Prime Minister at Chequers—all would have been well. Convoy protection would have got, say, the first five hundred four-engined planes on the grounds of urgency but thereafter most would go to Bomber Command because patrolling the Atlantic has a diminishing marginal utility and a low casualty rate whereas bombing Germany is the exact reverse. No such discussions ever took place or could take place. Heavy aircraft took off from land, land-based planes were exclusively vested in the RAF, it was for the RAF to decide how they were best employed. The first five hundred four-engined aircraft, they ordained, would have to go to Bomber Command. After June 1940, let's be honest, it was the only way we had to strike at the enemy.

The *next* five hundred would have to go to Bomber Command to make the force anywhere near effective; the five hundred *after that* would have to go to Bomber Command as replacements for planes shot down from the first two batches and, as they were being shot down rather a lot, every four-engined aircraft that came out of a British factory was required by Bomber Command until the end of the war. Naturally the air marshals were asked at frequent intervals how best they might contribute to the nerve-shredding Battle of the Atlantic and they replied on each and every occasion, "If only you would give us enough four-engined heavies, we'll knock out the submarine pens in France, plus the shipyards in Germany, and your problem will be solved at source." Which it was when the army captured the pens and the yards at the end of the war.

The navy never takes its defeats lying down and started plotting their next counterstroke against the RAF. They might have guessed aircraft were likely to be the answer to submarines because they had submarines of their own testifying to it. Alas! The one service the admirals disdained more than the army, the air force, the merchant navy and the Americans was their own Submarine Service. In any case, how could one deploy anti-submarine aircraft when all the anti-submarine aircraft belonged to the enemy?

One solution in the locker was *aircraft carriers* which most definitely could get planes out into the Atlantic though 'thanks to the RAF being in charge for the last twenty years' none of their planes would be suited to anti-submarine work when they got there. But the navy always copes and HMS *Courageous* (22,000 tons) was dispatched to take on 800-ton German submarines. Courageous did not find any U-boats but U-29 found Courageous. Scratch one flat-top.

Their next bright idea was the CAM, Catapult Aircraft Merchant ships. This involved putting a Hurricane fighter on a cargo vessel in the middle of a convoy and when a long range Focke-Wulf on reconnaissance for the U-boats appeared, the plane was catapulted off. This was some-times successful in dealing with Focke-Wulfs but always alarming for the Hurricane pilot who had a choice between ditching his plane or parachuting into the briny. Being a Fleet Air Arm navy pilot he was quite prepared to do either but the wider problem was the convoy now had to proceed on its way without air cover and the Focke-Wulf, dead or alive, had already summoned the U-boats.

This was all passing strange because the convoys were full of 'flat-tops'—oil tankers and bulk ore carriers ideally suited for conversion to allow basic take-off and landing. The Royal Navy was well aware of the concept because it had pioneered basic take-off and landing in the First World War by doing just that. The Admiralty thought not. They knew what a Second World War aircraft carrier looked like and it wasn't anything like a First World War prototype.

So the sinkings went on through 1939, 1940, 1941, 1942 and into 1943 at which point the Americans got involved. Up till then the US Navy had been relaxed about the sit-uation in the Atlantic. What they cared about was the

Pacific and their war against the US army, but in November 1942 the US army invaded North Africa and demanded something be done about getting them there safely. So the Americans lent the British some VLR (Very Long Range) Liberators, some expendable ('Jeep') escort carriers and the submarine menace was over.

*   *   *

30 Getting What You Wished For

The Royal Navy pulled off the tricky double of not only preparing for the wrong kind of war but coming off second best in the campaign they had been expecting.

Ever since the Anglo-Dutch Wars of the seventeenth century, the Royal Navy had prided itself on always having more ships than any other nation. To make sure, more than the two biggest other nations combined, a policy known as the Two Navy Rule. This was very expensive but it meant Rule Britannia over the seven seas, and that was very profitable. By the usual Curse of History the policy came to an end in 1919 just when the next biggest navy, Germany's, had scuttled itself *and* the British Empire had reached its territorial zenith. The sums were no longer adding up. From now on it was to be a One Navy Rule, the British must have a navy as big as the next biggest navy but need be no larger. The corollary of this policy, they soon discovered, was that while the Empire was everywhere, the Royal Navy could not be everywhere. The seven seas would have to come down by a digit or two.

The Pacific could be safely left to the Americans as there were not many British interests there and plenty of American ones. It was quite different in the Indian Ocean, lapping as it did the Suez Canal, the Gulf, the Raj, Malaya, Australia, South Africa, the very sinews of empire. No American interests, no American fleet, no prospects of American help and Japan to worry about. It now became evident why the two-navy policy had been so necessary. Your rivals did not have to gang up, they simply had to wait until your fleet was needed elsewhere. With the Germans rebuilding and the Italians threatening, the British were pondering their Japanese options.

In the first half of the twentieth century battleship design had gone through various peregrinations. At first, with the British HMS *Dreadnought*, it was simple enough. You stuck as many big guns (12-inch) on as you could, had as much armour protection against other big guns as you could, and off you went, blazing away. Much the same in fact as the way the Anglo-Dutch wars and all naval wars since had been fought. But one new factor was speed. There was no point in blazing away if your opponent was disappearing over the horizon and since the other fleet would, as a matter of policy, likely be smaller than the British fleet, it was all too likely to be disappearing over the horizon. So the British came up with the *battlecruiser* concept in time for the First World War. All the big guns (now 14 and 15 inch) as before but *faster* than a battleship. To achieve the speed the armour had to go so when your battlecruisers caught up with their battleships, your battlecruisers blew up after a few minutes of combat and their battleships resumed disappearing over the horizon.

After the Great War, the Germans found another solution with their *Scharnhorst* class. Very fast, very well armoured but, since something else had to give, not such big guns (11-inch). They were annihilated whenever they came up against ordinary 14-inch battleships. The Japanese concluded that *really* big was the answer and built two of the largest moving objects the world had ever seen, battleships with 18-inch guns. Sunk by submarines and airplanes respectively.

The British had stopped building battlecruisers in time for the Second World War but their new battleships turned out to be duds. On the first occasion they were called upon to fight other people's battleships, when the *Bismarck* came out in the spring of 1941, they discovered the Germans had squared the circle by putting in bigger engines. The Bismarck was a battlecruiser, with armour! To take on this innovatory leviathan, the British sent out two of their finest, the battlecruiser HMS *Hood*, 'the Pride of the Fleet', and their newest battleship, *Prince of Wales*. One salvo blew up the Hood, a few more forced the Prince of Wales to retire, and Bismarck disappeared over the horizon, shadowed by a pair of British (8-inch) cruisers.

The British called up their nearest aircraft carrier which mounted a textbook attack on the shadowing cruisers. Once this had been corrected the flukiest torpedo of the war jammed the Bismarck's rudder and she was obliged to sail round in circles while the British lumbered up with various heavy units pouring shot and shell into the hapless hulk. Still nothing. A cruiser had to be sent in to sink the Bismarck with torpedoes. The British accounted this a great victory which, like Jutland, it was because, despite being on the wrong end of so many technical shortcomings, at the end of the battle the British were there and the Germans were not. And never were again. Bismarck's sister, *Tirpitz*, was kept safely in its Norwegian fjord not least by four jolly jack tars putting explosives underneath her.

This was all largely irrelevant because battleships had come to the end of their four-hundred year reign as the arbiters of naval power, to be replaced by the aircraft carrier. This was not as clear then as in hindsight. The British had the unenviable record of losing the only direct battleship vs carrier engagement ever fought when the *Scharnhorst* sank HMS *Glorious* in 1940. Even so the Royal Navy had set about building, in its time-honoured fashion, more aircraft carriers than anyone else, and had achieved this by the start of the Second World War.

Neither the Germans nor the Italians had aircraft carriers which was luckier than the British knew because, just as the Dreadnought had wound the clock back to zero, allowing the Germans to build a rival battle fleet from scratch, so the advent of the aircraft carrier meant the Germans could have done the same again. They did not and for an all too familiar reason: the Luftwaffe controlled German air assets and there was no way they were going to allow the navy to win the war. The Italians viewed Italy as an unsinkable aircraft carrier in the middle of the Mediterranean and saw no need for the floating variety. British carriers took care of the Italian battleships in harbour at Taranto in 1940, showing the Japanese how to do it and their carriers took care of the American battleships at Pearl Harbour in 1941.

At the outset of war the decks were maybe cleared for the campaign the Admiralty had been planning for, taking on the Japanese. The Japanese were the *third*-ranking navy i.e. a lot of battleships, though not as many as the British, and a lot of aircraft carriers, though not as many as the British. The Royal Navy's scheme for taking on the Japanese was that Singapore would hold out long enough for the home fleet to sail halfway round the world to confront Japan in a grand Jutland-style battle. There was every prospect of success since the 18-inch behemoths were still in the shipyards and many of Japan's operational battleships and carriers were sclerotic. It might have seemed a rerun of Russia's campaign of 1904 when Port Arthur had

149

to hold out until the Russian fleet could sail round the world and that one was sunk without trace by the Japanese at Tsushima. But that was then, this is now.

We might speculate *now* what would have happened *then* if an unencumbered Royal Navy had actually fought the Japanese Combined Fleet as per Admiralty intentions. The battleships would never have engaged. Two hundred miles before any gun could be fired, the carrier aircraft would have fought out their battles and whoever won these would sink the battleships. But who would have won the carrier battle? The British with more and better carriers or the Japanese with not quite so many of either?

Undoubtedly it would have been the Japanese because of an obscure Royal Navy doctrine concerning the operation of planes at sea. British admirals held to the unshakeable view that pilots could not navigate over open ocean so they decreed that all carrier planes must have a navigator. What would have been a minor waste of manpower in normal circumstances was, at this particular juncture of British maritime aviation development, highly unfort- unate. The combination of a plane big enough for two, enough lift to get off a carrier deck and the uncaring RAF being in charge for twenty years meant *biplanes*. The Japanese were labouring under no such handicaps so, as the Royal Navy and the Imperial Japanese Navy steamed steadily towards one another, somewhere in between Brit- ish biplanes would have encountered Japanese Zeros with the fate of empires at stake. Oh dear.

Or maybe not. When the British next fought a naval war, in the Falklands, it was found that jump-jet Harriers could fly so slowly the Argentine jets found it impossible to shoot them down as they whooshed by, so perhaps the string- bags would have gone on to do a Midway rather than a

Tsushima. We will never know. What we do know is that when the Royal Navy finally did turn up in full battle array to take on the Japanese, after the defeat of Germany, they were hopeless. They managed the unusual feat, when taking on pilots committed to sacrificing themselves in one-way kamikaze flights, of losing twice as many aircraft as the enemy.

Not that anybody was taking much notice by this time. The entire British Pacific fleet was a sub-division of one of the US task forces. The Americans did not mind the British turning up with outdated methods but they minded like hell them turning up without a fleet logistics train. They had to cannibalise their task forces just to allow the Royal Navy to keep up.

*   *   *

31   How Intelligent Are Armies?

In modern societies there is a gulf between the military and the intelligentsia. This is not to say the military are unintelligent. Nor for that matter that the intelligentsia are intelligent, but it is safe to say the armed forces are not the first port of call for society's intellectual elite.

It was the Germans who first hit on the idea that, to the contrary, intellectuals are an essential component of any modern army. In the early nineteenth century, after yet another trouncing by the French, they came up with the notion of a *General Staff*, a body of men specially selected to think about war as opposed to fighting it. The success of German arms for the rest of the century led others to adopt the policy though for all anyone knew German soldiers were just better than everyone else's. By the twentieth century, all the Great Powers had their war colleges—the British had Sandhurst, the French Saint-Cyr—and all officers 'went to school' even if it was not the full General Staff indoctrination.

The British brought the trend to a pinnacle in the Second World War with *Operational Research*. The military men themselves were banished while groups of boffins worked out what was really going on in the fog of war, then told the soldiers what they ought to be doing instead. Actually *sailors* because Operational Research was inaugurated to address the submarine problem in the North Atlantic. The Operational Researchers would work out questions like the optimal number of ships in a convoy. Despite the safety of convoys being Britain's number one wartime problem nobody had ever crunched the numbers and it turned out to be eighty, far more than anyone had surmised.

Whether this was true in real life as opposed to on paper is doubtful. The effectiveness of mega-convoys could not be evaluated because by the time the British got round to applying the OR solution, the submarines had been dealt with and convoys of every size were getting through. Even if the OR people were correct and large convoys had been adopted in the dark days of 1940, eighty ships would have taken an age to assemble in Newfoundland and arriving together in Liverpool would have presented undreamt of opportunities for reserved occupation dockers. *That* problem would have to go all the way up to the war cabinet where Ernie Bevin, the dockworkers' leader, was in charge of sorting these things out.

The OR people were next tasked with finding the best depth charge setting for attacking submarines. This posed a different problem, the fog of war was affecting both sides. The British never suspected German submarines could go much deeper than anyone believed possible, much deeper than Blohm & Voss thought possible and they were building the wretched things. The U-boat captains had discovered it on a trial and error basis and weren't telling.

Operational Research has never fully taken off because military problems are rarely two-dimensional with limited variables (like convoys versus submarines) but so chaotically multivariate as to be beyond statistical analysis. Plus, even successful OR solutions can produce countermeasures worse than the original problem. It is all very well upping your game against submerging submarines but not if it prompts the other side to start using schnorkels, a pre-war Dutch invention that had been available all the time and which late in the war proved most effective. However, there is one type of campaign that *is* two-dimensional, *can* be statistically analysed and *won't* trigger later improvements. Global thermonuclear war. Over to you, boffins.

Hierarchical organisations are allegedly subject to the so-called Peter Principle

1. People who can do their jobs get promoted
2. People who can't do their jobs don't get promoted
3. In time all jobs are being done by people who can't do them

to which there are various objections

1. People who can't do their jobs get fired
2. People can make a good fist of any job from typist to CEO
3. People can be ham-fisted whether they are typists or CEO's
4. Organisations don't rely on the efficiency of their work force but construct rules of procedure that trained chimpanzees can follow.

It can be argued either way but there can be no argument that the armed forces in wartime will suffer the Peter Principle differently from run of the mill corporations (which include armed forces in peacetime).

Take the factor driving the whole Peter Principle: are incompetents sacked or are they left in post? We know the latter is common enough in every walk of life but the question is harder to resolve when those concerned are risking life and limb on a daily basis. Such people cannot help but be bands of brothers and applying the Peter Principle accordingly. This *may* lead to "Strewth, we'd better get this lot over by getting the square pegs into the square holes as quick as you like" but, given the way comrades in arms tend to think, it is more likely to be "He may be a donkey but he's a good chap, leave him where he is" or the more worrying "He may be a donkey but he's as brave as a lion, deserves a step up". On the other hand the armed forces can temper the Peter Principle because, being more rank-conscious than the average corporate body, they can shift people sideways 'retaining rank' until they land in a job they can do or it doesn't matter if they can't. There is also the mortality factor: promotion is markedly accelerated when a shell lands on the morning O-Group.

From time to time armed forces are obliged to come up with new, specialised units either to tackle an unforeseen problem posed by the enemy or to take advantage of a new technology of their own. By definition these units will have neither existing doctrine nor practical experience and will require particularly intelligent and flexible people. There is a set procedure:

1. A circular is sent out asking for suitable nominations to one of these new units
2. The circular drops onto the desk of the adjutant
3. "Do I put forward our most intelligent and flexible people, the ones that frankly are just about holding this battalion together?"
4. "Is this an opportunity to move on those deadbeats who cause me more grief than the rest of the battalion put together?"

The military does have one insoluble problem, operating in the two very different environments of peace and war. Those who are successful in peacetime conditions—working at a steady pace, expressing themselves well on paper, good with people, skilled in committee politics—rise to the

155

top, unavoidably filling the higher echelons when war breaks out and such qualities become less relevant. It requires the desk warriors to lose a few battles before they can be replaced by the unpleasant psychopaths who might get the job done.

Which brings us to the nub. Do we really want intelligent soldiers? Isn't this like having intelligent policemen? Wouldn't we rather have slightly stodgy coves in these dangerous roles? Dangerous to us, I mean, not the enemy. I don't want to end up speaking German but nor do I want to live in a police state under a military junta. I cannot give you an answer to this conundrum even though my own formative years were spent at Sandhurst. Sandhurst Road primary school, SE6.

*   *   *

32 Airborne Soldiers, Chairborne Generals

A Bridge Too Far, the film about the Arnhem campaign of September 1944, features many scenes of derring-do but is unsparing about the inadequacies of the British officer class. The title of the film itself points to flaws going right to the top but that is only half the picture. Arnhem also failed because of a lack of derring-do.

The ground war in the west was dominated by two immutable facts

1. The Germans were brilliant when it came to improvising defences
2. The Anglo-Americans were not brilliant when it came to improvising attacks

which meant the ground war in the west proceeded immutably along the following lines:

1. The British and Americans would mount a set-piece offensive using overwhelming force to score a complete battlefield victory resulting in an irresistible advance.
2. At some point the Germans would improvise a defence that resisted the advance.
3. The British and Americans would spend an indefinite period preparing their next move
4. a set-piece offensive using overwhelming force to score a complete battlefield victory.

The deciding factor was always the same: how long would it take the Allies to build up the 'overwhelming force'? It could take years, as with Normandy; it could take months, as with the North African landings; it could take weeks, as with Anzio. This last indicated that 'weeks' was probably not long enough. Arnhem was to be mounted in days. Which it was, superlatively well on the logistics side, but what was the hurry?

By September 1944 the Allies needed to cross the Rhine and decided that Arnhem was the place to do it. This was at first sight baffling because all that lay on the other side of the Rhine at Arnhem was northern Holland, an area of such minor strategic significance the Germans used it to rest up battered units. But, argued the Allied strategists, once across the Rhine, we can turn sharp right, surround the Ruhr and on to Berlin. Only the Arnhem bridges stand between us and final victory. They should have done their background checks.

The reason neither Britain nor the USA produce effective field armies is that, being maritime powers, they rarely get the practice. During their long and successful military careers, they have always tried to limit themselves to campaigns on islands, peninsulas and coastlines—places suited to small armies and big navies. They both avoid as far as possible 'traditional' military campaigns which are conducted on continental landmasses and require large armies and small navies. Hence, when the exigencies of foreign policy do demand the latter, they are chronically nervous about any type of operation that does not occur in the former. One such being opposed crossings of large rivers. English-speaking military men are convinced that major rivers are formidable hindrances for the attacking side whereas any continental general could have assured them such rivers are a problem *for the defenders.*

As one crossing point is mostly as good as another, the defending side has to protect the whole length of the river. In other words they will be widely dispersed along a fixed linear front and fixed linear fronts are best avoided because attackers can always

1. choose where to attack
2. concentrate overwhelming force at that point
3. break through with that overwhelming force
4. while the defence is still widely dispersed.

This being a standard military problem the defending side has a number of standard countermeasures

1. discover where the attack will take place by aggressive patrolling
2. interfere with the build-up using spoiling attacks
3. mount a counter-offensive before the attackers are ready

all of which are made tremendously difficult if there happens to be a major river in the way.

This is but the start of the defenders' difficulties. Concentrated offence against dispersed defence means a crossing can always be forced at some point, creating a salient on the defenders' side of the river. Standard armies have standard doctrines for pinching out standard salients which is *not* to attack front on (where the attackers are strongest), *not* to attack the shoulders of the salient (where the attackers are expecting them) but somewhere further out (the attackers cannot be strong everywhere). But again standard doctrine is in difficulties because anywhere they choose will require a river crossing. Meanwhile there is a salient to be urgently dealt with. Should the defenders decide to pinch the salient out directly they will have to use either neighbouring units or their reserves, handing the initiative back to the attackers who can choose between fighting it out in the salient or turning the main

159

attack into a feint by crossing the river in force somewhere else.

A lot of this applies to the attacking side as well and is why continental armies do not bother overmuch about rivers in the first place, whether attacking or defending them. Large rivers are useful for temporary regroupings in defence, they have to be taken into account like any other geographical feature on offence, but they are not to be obsessed over for months (even years) in advance and then dealt with by a panicky piece of rank adventurism when the time comes.

In September 1944, after their headlong advance across France, the Allies had once again run out of puff and the Germans had once again created a coherent defence line out of thin air. Montgomery chose this moment to act completely out of character. He was a very good British general (an appalling *Allied* general) because his style suited British methods and limitations. He would painstakingly build up a sufficient superiority of force to win a set-piece battle but, unlike many of his colleagues, he possessed a Ulysses S Grant-style ability to stick at it when things were not initially working, which was generally the case with the British army. After a successful local battle he would steadfastly refuse to jeopardise the gains by over-optimistic advances as British generals before him were in the habit of doing (or being sacked by Churchill if they didn't). Monty is often criticised for these strengths because military historians (e.g. Winston S. Churchill) are drawn to panache and celerity. It makes for more exciting books whether reading them, writing them or being brought up on them.

The Allies' task in September 1944 was clear enough. As their advance had stopped and German resistance had hardened, it was time for another lengthy pause while Allied superiority was built up. How was this best achieved? The entire campaign had been hampered because supplies were still for the most part coming across the Normandy beaches, so what was needed was a good working port somewhere right up near the front line. By great good fortune, Montgomery had just captured Antwerp, the finest port in the world for shifting supplies from Britain and America into the heart of Europe. Of course the Germans knew this too so while they had surrendered Antwerp without a fight, they had strengthened the defences along the Lower Scheldt, Antwerp's link to the sea, meaning ships could not reach the city until the Scheldt was cleared. Again by great good fortune, an entire Anglo-American army (the Canadians) was standing by, and they had considerable experience of amphibious landings.

It should be explained that the Canadian government had decided in 1939 that they must fight as a separate army so Canadian soldiers spent the first five years of the war inactive while enough Canadians could be assembled to form a separate army. They were given the disastrous two-day Dieppe landings in 1942 to see how they were getting along, a forlorn campaign along the Adriatic coast in 1943 and their own beach on D-Day in 1944, but basically they were raring to go. It only required the green light for the Canadians to clear the Scheldt, Antwerp to be opened up and the advance into Germany could resume. Montgomery decided this was just the opportunity he needed to show his critics he was not a stodgy set-piece commander but a dashing latter-day Rupert of the Rhine. He green-lighted the Anglo-American Arnhem campaign instead of the Canadian Scheldt campaign. Eisenhower, with a stodgy reputation of his own to live down, not to mention a chronic inability to control subordinate commanders, green-lighted the green light.

The basic premise of Operation Market Garden (*Market* was the airborne component, *Garden* the simultaneous ground advance) was that the elite British XXX Corps would drive seventy miles north from the Dutch border to the Rhine using intermediate river crossings captured by airborne forces along the way. The ground troops were all British, the airborne half-and-half British and American. The Americans were by now familiar with British warfighting methods and insisted the nearby bridges were assigned to their airborne and the more distant ones, the Arnhem bridges across the Rhine itself, were to be given to British paras. The Limeys might get their act together to reach their boys, relieving our boys along the way. A wise prognostication.

There was a good airborne landing zone right next to the Arnhem bridges but it was presenting the British with a problem. German flak guns guarding the bridges would be a severe hazard for slow-moving transport planes, worse for gliders and downright lethal for soldiers floating down on parachutes. This is not an unexpected situation for airborne troops to find themselves in since any objective meriting an airborne assault is likely to be heavily defended and there was standard doctrine for dealing with it

1. Use tactical aircraft to run flak suppression sorties which, as the Allies by this stage of the war had thousands of tactical aircraft, could be done

2. Accept a certain amount of casualties which, as the Allies by this stage of the war were a bunch of pussies, could not be done.

This is most unfair of course and definitely did not apply to British and American paratroopers who were uniformly excellent, but Anglo-Americans are congenitally averse to certain *kinds* of casualties, the kind that gets the attention of newspaper-reading democracies. Losing hundreds of men in an opposed river crossing to capture a vital bridge-head earns a promotion, losing hundreds of men riddled with bullets as they float down on parachutes to capture the same bridgehead gets the sack.

The British airborne troops were dropped (without casualties) eight miles outside Arnhem, then lost many men (and a lot of time) fighting their way to the bridges. Actually *bridge*, the Germans had plenty of time to blow all the Arnhem bridges but left one intact in case they might want it themselves for a counter-offensive. This in itself did not affect Market Garden. The point about river crossings is that the attackers do not have to physically capture bridges, always a rarity, but so long as one's troops are established on the other side, new crossings can be constructed in typically a day and a night. In order to cross the Rhine all that was required was for the British airborne troops to occupy the northern bank of the Rhine long enough for XXX Corps to reach the southern bank, plus a day and a night. This seemed feasible because Market Garden envisaged XXX Corps reaching the south bank opposite Arnhem in two days and, in the event, the British airborne forces were able to hold the north bank for nine.

The reason the airborne held out so long, why they had to hold out so long, is not quite as the books (and the film) would have us believe. The German commander, Model, is portrayed as a blundering ignoramus, not just caught nap-ping by the British descent on Arnhem (where he actually had his HQ) but dismissing it as unimportant. That'll teach him to underestimate the military finesse of the Allies.

He was indeed surprised but Model was not called 'Hitler's Fireman' for nothing. He is widely regarded as the best defensive general produced by the Second World War so he may be worth listening to. His appreciation of the situation was that the airborne troops could be left to wither on the vine (which they did) while he concentrated on delaying XXX Corps (which he did). If the Allies really wanted to mount their major autumn offensive to create a seventy-mile, one-road wide, salient overlooked the whole way by his own forces enjoying possibly the world's best road/rail infrastructure on the Dutch-Belgian-German borders, they could be his guest (which they were for the rest of the war).

What he would *not* be needing were the two SS arm-oured divisions that were, unbeknownst to the Allies, refitting near Arnhem and which the books, the film and the national consciousness blame for the overall but glorious failure of Market Garden. Imagine! A bedraggled collection of parachutists holding off two armoured div-isions of the Waffen SS for nine whole days. Makes you proud.

Of our ability to spin heroic myths from so little yarn and was only one of many spectres haunting our collective memory of the Arnhem campaign:

1. Model was the most nazified of the top German generals—he committed suicide in April 1945—so he is not permitted any role that casts him in other than a poor light.

2. SS panzer divisions are not all they are cracked up to be. Even when operational they might not have fifty 'runners' but in September 1944 it is doubtful if these particular divisions had any tanks at all, apart from those 'refitting'. The Germans could not afford to keep working tanks in rest and recreation areas.

3. Mr Daphne du Maurier (General 'Boy' Browning, the overall airborne commander) is clearly an upper class twit with connections. His remark that the biggest airborne campaign in history should *not* be halted because aerial reconnaissance reported three panzers hiding behind a hedge is taken as downright incompetence. It certainly would have been.

4. Robert Redford was unavailable. The Americans tasked with capturing the vital Nijmegen crossings across the Waal dropped only on one side of the river and had omitted to bring any boats with them so had to wait for the bemused British to arrive with some.

5. The British were not 'stopping for tea', as the Americans angrily claimed, when Britain's future Foreign Secretary refused to send unsupported tanks on a suicide mission in broad daylight up a single road without cover in the face of prepared anti-tank defences.

6. Though he did later lose us the Falklands.

Even so the plan worked in principle. When XXX Corps finally arrived on the south bank of the Rhine, their airborne comrades were still established on the north bank. After a hasty conflab the armoured units declined to cross in the face of a nine-day build-up of German defences. Actually XXX Corps could have crossed for all the Germans cared since staring at British spearheads can be done as easily on one side of a river as the other. That is the whole point: no sensible army would choose a schwerpunkt in the middle of featureless polderland mud facing dry-shod opponents with a fabulous communication system at their back. Even the Allied commanders understood there was no alternative but to withdraw the surviving paratroopers who paddled back across the Rhine in fine style. The British are textbook retreaters.

True, had the plan worked to its original timetable and an entire British armoured corps had been established on the German side of the Rhine in forty-eight hours or so, the Germans would have been thoroughly discommoded—they might have to put a rush order on those refitting tanks—so it is essential to know why this did not happen. The British armoured formations had to advance across a flat marshy terrain, obliged to use a limited number of roads, devoid of cover but elevated just enough to be ideal targets for German anti-tank guns. No wonder the road from the Belgian border to Arnhem was dubbed 'Hell's Highway'.

When devising the plan presumably somebody could read a map, count the roads and measure the elevation. "I say, sir, better not go that way, it'll be a regular hell's highway." But if anyone had, it would have been answered with "Don't be so defeatist, haven't we spent most of our war driving across flat deserts with very few roads, no cover and just enough elevation for Germans taking potshots at us?" Nobody heard the oik pushing in the tea trolley mutter, "We never solved that one either."

*   *   *

33 First Rule of Fight Club

As a British revisionist historian it pains me to say so but Churchill was the best of the war leaders. This was not all down to him personally, the British system was the best for warmaking purposes. It does need a vigorous personality to operate and this often requires a change at the top—Devonshire to Pitt, Aberdeen to Palmerston, Asquith to Lloyd George, Chamberlain to Churchill—but once it gets going the British system delivers what is necessary in the unique pressures of total war.

A requirement of a war leader is to be in control of the armed forces: standing above them, apportioning resources among them, between them and allied forces, between military and civilian needs. All governments in theory stand above the service chiefs but in wartime staying on top demands special measures. Stalin's preferred solution, shooting them, is not the best way. Not the worst either but service chiefs do need reining in because they are surprisingly bad when it comes to wider war policy. They either rise to the top in peacetime (different set of skills entirely) or they rise to the top as battlefield commanders (different set of skills entirely) but they always rise to the top in *one* of the services, giving them incorrigibly monocular vision about which service is best placed to do what and to whom.

Churchill had the good luck, or the good judgement, to have Alanbrooke, the professional head of the British army, as his chief adviser, and Alanbrooke was the one true strategic genius produced by the war. Not least in his ability to deal with Churchill. The point about the British system is that when there is somebody with 'grip' at the top, things run smoothly. The civilian departments—the Foreign Office, Exchequer, Food and the rest—have sufficient weight to ensure that the three service ministries (and, in the British system, the war supply ministries) do not run the show. This is the essence of 'cabinet government' and only Britain had it in any effectual form. Churchill made himself Minister of Defence as well as Prime Minister to make sure the cabinet itself did not run the show.

But the true test of a War Leader is *how* the armed forces are deployed, what is known as Grand Strategy. In this, Churchill had a patchy record. His first big decision, to send reinforcements to the Middle East in 1940 when Britain was itself in imminent danger of invasion, proved to be correct, if dangerously precipitate. Wisdom is not always equatable with outcome. On the other hand, having done so, his insistence on a Mediterranean strategy right up until June 1944 was surely correct as it was the one theatre in which British and American armies could hope to tie down German armies with any prospect of success. Churchill can also be exonerated for the strategically irrelevant campaign in Burma since, as he recognised but later commentators often do not, the chief war aim in the east was not the defeat of Japan but the re-establishment of the British Empire.

Churchill's failures though are substantial. He did not attend to the Battle of the Atlantic sufficiently despite this being, as he put it, the only thing that kept him awake at night. Certainly he was let down by his professional advisers but given his naval background in both world wars he ought to have sacked admirals (notably the serially incompetent and chronically ailing First Sea Lord, Dudley Pound) as promptly as he sacked generals. One cannot help suspecting this was *because* of Churchill's naval background. He could bully Pound with impunity and the Admiralty was the one service department that made operational decisions in London. Playing with ships is irresistible when you cannot play with soldiers.

On the air front, his support for strategic bombing was as unwavering as was his scepticism about its real importance. Political more than strategic.

Churchill's biggest failings were where British *fighting* assets were to be deployed. Far too many divisions, far too many destroyers, far too many fighter planes were held in readiness at home when there was little direct danger from Germany after the invasion of Russia. These wasted assets in Britain paled when set against the half-million British 'static troops' (i.e. other than the Eighth Army) that spent the whole war in the Middle East guarding against vague and increasingly unlikely contingencies. On the single occasion this half-million was called on to fight Germans, in the Dodecanese in 1943, they were seen off inside a week by a few thousand German static troops. Elsewhere there was a chronic shortage of infantry on every British fighting front.

Despite the constitutional provisions, the USA does not have cabinet government nor, in the Second World War, did it have a commander-in-chief. Their system is essentially an elected monarchy and the monarch cannot be replaced just because a war comes along. They are stuck with whoever happens to be in the White House and in December 1941 Roosevelt was a burnt-out case. He did not have 'grip'. Even his old department, the Navy, was left to run its own private war in the Pacific, making its own strategic decisions. The army too went its own way in the Pacific under the very weird MacArthur. In fact the whole Pacific War was operated as a contest between the US Navy (including the Marine Corps) and the US Army (not including the strategic Army Air Force). The airmen thought they should be independent like the RAF and this ambition was largely achieved under the American system of combined planning. Press release combined with pork barrel. Newsworthy raids and an airplane plant in every state soon had ten per cent of American war output being devoted to building USAAF bombers though, unlike the army and the navy, they did at least win the Pacific War, at Hiroshima and Nagasaki. Or so the press releases said. The RAF's own Bomber Command was taking a *third* of British output but, right or wrong, this was at least down to Churchillian belligerence rather than Rooseveltian indolence.

Roosevelt left the European theatre to Marshall who left it to Alanbrooke. Marshall and Alanbrooke made an odd couple. Both were professional heads of their army, both were chief advisers on overall war policy, but their talents went in opposite directions. Marshall was a brilliant administrator but quite out of his depth in strategy. Americans are always out of their depth in strategy because, lacking neighbours posing a strategic threat, they never acquire the antibodies. Whenever a strategic threat does come along, say, in the form of the Japanese bombing of Pearl Harbour or militant Islam's bombing of the Twin Towers, they unleash everybody they can think of against anybody they can think of and hope for the best.

The Japanese were to be corralled from every conceivable direction by every conceivable armed service. The army was to plod northwards through the worst imaginable terrain of New Guinea and the Philippines, launch themselves somewhere onto the China coast and finally invade the Japanese home islands. The navy was to island-hop westwards until it met up with the army somewhere on the China coast and take it over to Japan. The airforce was to reposition itself fifteen hundred miles from Burma to the China coast ready to join its sister services for the final leap except it was not clear how because Japan kept occupying the airfields at one end and the Americans kept building roads to nowhere at the other. Still, it all looked terrific on the newsreels with those big black arrows moving inexorably towards the lair of the beast.

Meanwhile the submarine campaign on its own was rendering Japan strategically prostrate. The Japanese could do no more than stay where they were and kill as many people placed in front of them as they could. The US Navy complied with this request by using up thousands of marines in a step-by-step advance taking every Japanese outpost but realised after a while there was no point in eliminating Japanese garrisons that could not feed them-selves never mind pose a threat to anyone else, so they started hopping *over* islands.

MacArthur had vowed 'I shall return' after being driven out of the Philippines at the start of the war when he only had a three-to-two superiority, and made sure that tens of thousands of Americans and hundreds of thousands of Filipinos would pay for a promise kept. Why was he allow-ed to do so? Roosevelt may not have been a great war leader but he was a great politician. Why risk a disgruntled MacArthur running against you in 1944 as McClellan did against Lincoln in 1864?

Grossly unfair no doubt because Roosevelt did get the One Big Decision right: the war against Germany must take priority over the war with Japan. This may be Grand Strategy 101—Germany being a global threat, Japan a regional one—but this is not how an enraged American electorate viewed matters the day after the Day of Infamy. It took political courage of a high order to persuade them of the wisdom of Germany First. The courage and the wisdom did not last long. South Pacific was playing to such packed houses and An American in Paris was so long in production that resources were soon heading westwards on a scale that meant starvation rations (by American standards) for the European theatre. D-Day had to be postponed because nobody could persuade the US Navy to disgorge the landing craft it needed to gold plate the invasion of some tropical atoll or other.

Theoretically the Japanese followed the British system—a constitutional monarch, a prime minister and a cabinet—but a minor, apparently innocuous, local convention made all the difference. Japanese cabinets had to include a representative from both the army and the navy. Nothing surprising there, the British and Americans had similar arrangements, but the Japanese introduced a novelty—the representatives had to be a *serving* soldier and a *serving* sailor. Nothing wrong with that either, the brightest Japanese brains often wanted to fight for their country. As cabinet members they naturally advocated policies favourable to the army and navy, as of course did their British and American counterparts. They might even resign if they did not get their way, something that also happens in Britain and America, but now comes the twist. Serving soldiers and sailors in any country are part of a chain of command so if they did not get their way and resigned, *they could not be replaced*. Their successors would also be

172

serving soldiers/sailors, also advocating these policies, also threatening to resign if they were not adopted, and so on ad infinitum. Since every government had to have a soldier and a sailor Japan could either have a de facto military government or no government at all.

This is not bad in itself, military governments are not per se better or worse than civilian ones, but this was not military government in the ordinary sense. It was government by army *and* navy. Each had a veto, each had to be satisfied and Japan was not America, they could not both be satisfied. Somebody else would have to pay. By the late thirties that reliable treasure chest, China, was actually costing money and there were no prospects in Russia, so where? The army reckoned the south-east Asian mainland fitted the bill, the navy thought the south-east Asian islands were a better prospect, so they compromised and attacked both. This meant the navy would be up against the world's two largest navies, the British and the American, and the army would be up against the world's two largest armies, the Chinese and the Russian but, like I say, Grand Strategy is not an armed forces forte.

Besides, the Japanese seemed to regard rationality as cheating, not a proper test of the banzai spirit. That said, the campaigns of 1941-2 were exemplary exercises in minimum force and combined planning as Malaya, Burma, the Philippines, Indonesia and the South Pacific islands were taken despite, on every occasion, being up against superior forces. The banzai spirit really does work which is why less foolhardy nations, when confronted by Japan, switch from 'superior forces' to 'overwhelmingly superior forces'.

Stalin's Admiral Byng policy had a significant addendum: don't always shoot them, send some to the gulag. That way you can suddenly free them, catapult them back to high office and see how they get on. It says much for the human spirit that the generals (and the armament designers) returned from exile with redoubled enthusiasm and enhanced acuity. Working once more for this curiously capricious employer was a real tonic for emaciated bodies and hollow staring eyes. Perhaps a spell in Leavenworth would have made Eisenhower a more forceful commander.

Stalin had the easiest military decisions to make—one enemy, one front—and did his best to muck it up. He got the wrong enemy (Germany in June 1941) and fought them on the wrong front (the new Polish frontier rather than the long-prepared defences in Byelorussia) but these decisions were self-righting. After confining himself to his dacha for several weeks with a nervous breakdown on hearing of the German invasion, Stalin returned to the Kremlin with redoubled enthusiasm and enhanced acuity. Alone among the war leaders, he was a professional bureaucrat and rapidly decided who was to get what:

1. Red Army everything, navy and air force nothing
2. armed forces everything, civilians nothing
3. Soviet Union everything, allies nothing.

But what of his record as a Grand Strategist? Stalin is quite undeservedly criticised for not anticipating the German attack. He did anticipate it, he anticipated nothing else, but he could not have anticipated it happening in June 1941. Intelligence of German intentions was flooding in from all sides, intelligence always floods in from all sides, and all sides wanted him to believe a German attack was imminent. The western powers would be only too happy if their two chief antagonists set about fighting one another; it suited Japan; even the Germans were not averse to

174

having Stalin think they *might* attack since it strengthened their diplomatic and economic demands. Russia alone did not want it and in those nervous times there was nothing like preparing for a war to precipitate it. That was precisely what had happened in 1914 when Germany had precipitated the First World War because a re-arming Russia needed to be forestalled. And secret intelligence? Pah! Stalin knew more about secret intelligence than anyone in the whole wide world.

Even so it was a mistake and not his last. He over-insured by keeping too many troops in the Far East but, considering the Japanese propensity for surprise attacks, this could be viewed as erring on the side of caution. Not at all. It is a common mistake in times of crisis to err on the side of caution but crises are crises because erring in any direction can be fatal. The Battle of Moscow was won by a whisker when Far Eastern forces were belatedly summoned.

Or so the history books say. Lenin claimed 'Communism is Soviet Power plus Electricity' but the Germans discovered the relevant equation was 'Soviet Power equals Russia plus Communism' because no matter how many millions of soldiers were thrown away by Stalin's blunders, no matter how vast the territories lost to the Wehrmacht, the Russians still won by a landslide. You cannot beat communism on the battlefield. Aside from the first against Poland in 1920, and the last against Afghanistan in 1989, no communist country has ever lost a war to a non-communist country. Never vote for them, never fight against them.

Administratively Hitler was the most interesting of the war leaders. This is because of a singular method he employed, the *Führerprinzip*. Despite suspicions this was to compensate for his own pronounced laziness when it came to paperwork, the success of both the German war machine and the economy that underpinned it suggests this way of operating state machinery is worth a second look. Hitler himself gave an example of how the Führerprinzip works. In the early days of the Party somebody wrote to him to say the local organisation was in the hands of (a) someone with no qualifications except (b) a lengthy criminal record whereas (c) he was a lawyer with (d) a large motorcar for ferrying brownshirts around and (e) a house big enough for local party meetings so would (f) Hitler do something about it? Hitler wrote back, 'If you can oust him you will have my complete backing. If not, I'm sure there are other ways you can support the party.'

The Führerprinzip operates at all levels of administration. People have to fight amongst themselves in a conscious reflection of Hitler's favourite biological theory, the survival of the fittest. Of course it may only have been the famed efficiency of the German civil service and armed forces that was really carrying the nation but we are not allowed to critique Nazi methods with the requisite discernment to find out. Possibly a good thing when it comes to world domination but it might be useful when analysing that other Nazi speciality, emerging from economic slumps in double quick time. It may have been Germany's ruthless devil-take-the-hindmost approach to international trade, giving everybody else a Keynesian kick up the backsides, that did the trick, but we shall never know. Supping with the devil is not permitted unless it can be done on the quiet, for instance by using data from concentration camp medical experiments in the aerospace industries after the war. Good. They did not die entirely in vain.

We can though infer how the Führerprinzip operated from the varying fortunes of the leading personalities of the Third Reich. Take, by way of example, the ups and downs of Herman Goering. Goering was an energetic and successful politician of the twenties and thirties, forcing his way to power second only to Hitler when the Nazis took office (by constitutional and democratic means, though this is not a popular case study for psephologists). Goering was rewarded with or helped himself to—it is always difficult to tell with the Führerprinzip—two critical government jobs: economic overlord as head of the Four Year Plan *and* in charge of the Luftwaffe. These would normally be incompatible, the Luftwaffe would get undue preference when resources were being shared out, but as Hitler would have put it if he had thought about it at all, the Luftwaffe needed to be hot-housed in competition with the established Army and Navy. It took some of the democracies ages to reach the same conclusion.

As an old fighter pilot himself, Goering figured that another fighter ace, Ernst Udet, should be put in charge of aviation development. But that is perhaps a criticism of the Führerprinzip. Just as Goering himself descended into lethargy and drug addiction faced with the uncongenial life of the official, so Udet spiralled down into despair and suicide knowing how much he had ruined the Luftwaffe with a series of terrible planes. Never mind, the Führerprinzip delivered up Erhard Milch, an authentic bureaucratic genius, and the Luftwaffe was once more overtaking the world in technical development.

Goering's economic hold was soon loosened by his own inaction (that is also the way the Führerprinzip works) and Fritz Todt found himself in charge of large slices of German military industry. Very efficient he was too but he had no party backing so was regularly outbid for resources by people with louder voices at Hitler's court. However, as the climax of the war approached in 1942, the Führerprinzip swung into action. Todt was killed in an air crash and replaced by Albert Speer, the nearest to a friend Hitler ever had. Whether Speer was any better than Todt as an administrator is immaterial, he had the ear of Hitler, hence so too did the war economy which rocketed upwards, disconcerting the Allies who thought they were bombing Germany back to the Stone Age.

Perhaps the most remarkable of the Führerprinzip results was that the German armed forces kept right on doing what they were told (the July plotters apart) until the very end. The whole German population did. This is not, as is often charged, the German way. In 1918 both the generals and the populace gave up as soon as it was unmistakeable which way the wind was blowing and before any foreign army had even reached Germany. Hitler must have been doing something wrong.

However, it is Hitler as War Leader that is the acid test. He was certainly one of the most incompetent grand strategists *and* military commanders ever put in charge of a Great Power but this is to judge him by the wrong yardstick. The two people who most enjoyed the war were Hitler and Churchill, both adored playing with soldiers. This did not matter much in the case of Churchill because firstly he was constrained by the system he was operating (Hitler wasn't) and secondly British forces were not material to the outcome of the war (Germany's were). It is all very well saying it was a gross military error having large German armies in Norway, the Balkans, North Africa and Italy but these were *Hitler's* campaigns not Germany's. The Kaiser did not conduct twice-daily briefings, with him

doing the briefing. Launching a new campaign might provide Hitler with a pick-me-up but he was not the least
downcast when the tide of war turned and it was the Allies
launching the new campaigns. He just switched roles. He
was now the Iron Corporal.

The Führerprinzip applies as much to the Führer as to
anyone else. The campaign that decided the war, in Russia,
would have to go to the General Staff. Hitler's solution?
Two general staffs of course. The OKH for the professionals in Russia and the OKW for himself everywhere
else. Both in the end were unsuccessful but criticising Hitler's *militarily* ridiculous policy of no strategic withdrawals
is once again to miss the point. What difference did it
make to him whether Germany lost in the spring or the
autumn of 1945 if it meant it was him playing at soldiers
rather than those moaning minnies over in the Bendlerstrasse? No, Hitler had a very successful war.

*   *   *

34 Last Knockings

Towards the end of the war four of the five main combatants developed revolutionary long-range weapons. The
odd one out discovered, in the brave new world of techno-
logical innovation, it can pay to come second.

The Germans produced the world's first ballistic missile,
a tribute either to innate German genius or innate Anglo-
French stupidity. The Versailles Treaty of 1919 forbade the
Germans military aircraft so they set about developing any
form of air warfare not requiring military aircraft. After
the glider and the cruise missile, they came up with the V2
which weighed thirteen tons, reached the edge of space,
used up the last vestiges of the German war economy and
killed between one and two persons per rocket. It was
possibly the least cost-efficient weapon of war ever
invented.

The Japanese long-range weapon was more ambitious
than the V2 in having full intercontinental capability but
less advanced in being a paper balloon with an explosive
tied underneath. It was released from the Japanese homeland to float across the Pacific and land in North America.
An over-curious dog in Oregon was badly frightened. It
was possibly the least efficient weapon of war ever invented.

The Anglo-Americans, hereinafter known as the Americans, came up with a weapons package consisting of a B-
29 with an atomic bomb tied underneath. This produced
fifty thousand deaths per unit deployed and was possibly
the most efficient weapon of war ever invented.

The Russians looked upon these developments with their usual mix of envy, fear and avarice. They acquired rockets from the Germans by kidnap, atomic bombs from the Americans by espionage, stuck the one on top of the other and produced possibly the most efficient weapon of war not invented.

*   *   *

35 Who Won The War?

August 1945 saw the event that finally brought the Second World War to an end. Not Hiroshima, not Nagasaki, but something else entirely. Something which, to this day, all parties have been careful to ignore. The relevant sequence of events was

1. Feb 1945: Yalta Conference. Anglo-Americans request Russia join the war against Japan. Stalin agrees to do so six months after the surrender of Germany
2. March-April: At Allied urging, Stalin agrees to cut this to three months
3. 8th May: Germany surrenders
4. 6th August: Americans drop atomic bomb on Hiroshima
5. 8th August: Russia declares war on Japan as agreed
6. 9th August: Americans drop atomic bomb on Nagasaki
7. 15th August: Japan surrenders.

The assumption is that (7) followed from (4) and (6) but Japanese records indicate this was not the case. Although the atomic bombs caused cataclysmic megadeaths, these events were treated by the Japanese war cabinet as no more than 'major casualties caused apparently by a new weapon'. This stoicism was entirely normal. The conventional fire-bombing of Tokyo in March 1945 had produced twice, perhaps three times, the number of deaths as either Hiroshima or Nagasaki without affecting Japanese resolve to carry on fighting. For Japan, as for Germany and for Britain, civilian casualties just did not figure in issues of war or peace.

It is true the Japanese had been sending out peace feelers, only to be expected given the way the war was going, but they were not 'suing for peace'. Japan was fully prepared to let go most, not all, of her overseas conquests but there was not the remotest chance of the Japanese accepting the only terms on offer from the Anglo-Americans: unconditional surrender followed by an indefinite occupation of their country. And why would they? The Americans would soon be talking more realistically faced with the scale of casualties required to invade the Home Islands (a million, thought the Americans; a lot more than that, thought the Japanese). The Japanese were not to know their peace proposals had no chance of success anyway as they were being conveyed via the Russians who wanted the war to continue until their own entry into it. It was that entry that changed Japanese minds.

The Pacific War is always viewed as a largely USA versus Japan business but the raw numbers do not reflect this. About a quarter of Japan's military forces were ranged against the Americans, another quarter were opposing the British and the remaining half were in China either fighting the Chinese or being held in readiness against the Russians. Looked at from the other side, the hopeless old moth-eaten British Empire was putting twice the numbers into the field as the Americans.

Russia's Manchurian campaign of August 1945, as well as being possibly the least acknowledged episode of the war, had its most unexpected result. By this stage everything that could be known about the capabilities of the various armies was thought to be known. For example, the Japanese had consistently proved to be better man-for-man than both the Americans and the British, yet man-for-man the Red Army destroyed the Japanese Kwantung Army in a few days. The shock to the Japanese was absolute. Losing battles in faraway places to Anglo-American matériel could be borne, having their main field army swept aside by the Russians (the Russians!) shattered the Japanese martial spirit. Centuries of uninterrupted military success and they were paper tigers after all.

The military, hitherto advocates of war at any cost, now insisted on peace at any cost. This is not so unusual—the exact same sequence of events had played out in 1918 after the German General Staff had received *their* first ever defeat. Military men are like that: they don't give a stuff about the nation's suffering but when it's them that are suffering, the nation must suffer peace.

One last mystery remains to be cleared up. Why, to this day, has the ending of the best-documented war in history been so misrepresented? Each belligerent had a choice of explanation for the sudden end to hostilities: was it the American bomb or the Russian army? The Japanese, writing up their war memoirs, could figure it either way:

1. Japan had fought a surprisingly successful sea-based campaign against the world's two greatest naval powers but once these immensely larger nations were fully mobilised, Japan was obliged to make a step-by-step fighting withdrawal to the home islands whereupon the Anglo-Americans, rather than face the fearsome casualties an aroused nation would inflict on them, concocted the most vile weapon in the history of mankind and used it not once but twice on a defenceless civilian population. The Emperor and his ministers decided that to spare their people further catastrophes Japan would have to give best to her assailants. To be perfectly honest, the Japanese were the *victims* in all this.

2. The Japanese were brutal expansionists, initially successful by duplicity, turned back decisively by the Anglo-Americans and ultimately defeated with contemptuous ease by the Russians.

Let's go with *ichi*. The Americans had a similar choice:

1. It was the atomic bombs that finally did for Japan. After nearly four years of battling the Japanese across the Pacific, American armed forces had reached islands close enough for direct bombing of the Japanese mainland culminating in Hiroshima and Nagasaki, forcing Japan's unconditional surrender. There could only be one seat at the peace conference and the good old US of A would be sitting in it.

2. It took the Russians and their Manchurian campaign to make Japan give up. Strictly speaking, the whole Pacific War was superfluous since it was obvious the Russians would have won anyway. There would, it seems, have to be two seats at the peace conference and the Russians would be staring at them across the table.

The Americans took the Nuclear Option. That left the Russians (the British and the Chinese were US puppets) to decide how the war ended:

1. Of no concern whatsoever was a seat at the peace table. After Tehran, Yalta and Potsdam, they did not want any more yapping from the British and Americans about free and fair elections. Free and fair elections always seemed to go the Anglo-American way whenever it was their boots on the ground so let's get some Soviet boots into the northern half of Korea, the southern half of Sakhalin and why not pop the Kuriles in the bag while we're about it? One reason might be unwavering Japanese hostility putting a giant spanner in one's global foreign policy

185

for the next seventy years but Russians take other people hating them as a given in foreign policy.

2. What did concern them was the Americans having the Bomb and only one conceivable country to drop it on. Without a Bomb of their own they would have to rely on TASS. The first thing was to draw the world's attention to the frightfulness of atomic weapons and the people who used them. So frightful it forced the Japanese to surrender. We *know*, we were brokering peace talks on their behalf at the time. The Americans could have waited a week or two but no doubt they wanted to conduct some live experiments with their new toy.

With everyone agreed it was the atomic bombs dropped on Hiroshima and Nagasaki that brought about the Japanese surrender, that is officially how the Second World War ended. As does this account of it.

INDEX

ASDIC 138, 140
A Bridge Too Far 157
Aberdeen, Lord 167
Abteilung 70
Abyssinia (Ethiopia) 5, 6
Académie Française 61
ace 77-83, 177
  air 77, 78, 80-2
  American 77, 78
  British 77, 78
  French 77
  German 78, 79
  Italian 82
  Japanese 78, 79-82
  Russian 77-8
  tank 78
  U-boat 78
  Wittman, Michael 78
adjutant 155
administration
  American 170
  British 94, 141
  German 68, 176-8
  Russian 59
admiral 123, 137-8, 141, 143,
      150, 168, 174
Admiralty 135, 140, 149-50, 169
  First Lord 32, 94
  First Sea Lord 94, 168
  incompetence of 137-8, 144
Adriatic 161
advance
  American 157, 161, 171
  axes of 24
  British 72, 76, 157, 160, 161, 166
  crossing the T 70-1
  German 24, 28, 36, 72, 120
  tank 64, 67, 70, 72, 166
advisers 42, 167, 168, 170
Afghanistan 39, 56, 134, 175
Africa 5
  Central 110
  North 35, 65, 85, 118, 145, 157, 178
  South 45, 105, 146
  West 38
Afrika Korps 119
agent, secret 125, 126
air 57, 74, 85, 141-3, 147, 149, 169, 180
  aces 77, 78, 80-2
  anti- 75, 81, 141
  bases 41
  battle 78, 84, 142
  -borne 56-7, 128, 157-66
  combat 89
  -craft (see airplanes)
  crew 89, 92, 142

  field 171
  marshall 54, 141, 143
  -men 92, 141, 142, 170
  -mindedness 84-8
  Ministry 122
aeroplane (see airplane)
air forces 86, 92, 143
  American 87, 89, 170, 171
  British 87, 89, 92, 123, 141-3, 170
  Fleet Air Arm 141, 151
  German 89, 142, 149, 180
  Russian 174
  support 74, 86
  tactical 84, 87
aircraft (see airplane)
aircraft carrier 148-9, 150
  American 78, 80, 81
  British 144, 145, 148-9, 150
  German 149
  Italian 149
  Japanese 78, 80, 81, 82, 149,
      150
airplane (inc aircraft, plane) 56, 77, 80,
      84, 85, 89, 92, 140-144,
      147, 150, 177, 180
  anti-submarine 140, 142-4
  biplane 150
  bomber (see main entry)
  carrier (see aircraft carrier)
  courier 22
  fighter 80-81, 89, 90, 91, 92, 169
  four-engined 142, 143
  gliders 162, 180
  jets 123, 150
  kamikaze 81, 151
  modern 27
  tactical 74, 75, 84, 87, 162
  tank-busting 70
  transport 162
    see also individual planes
    B-17 89-90, 91-2
    B-29 180
    Flying Fortress (see B-17)
    Focke-Wulf 144
    Halifax 90
    Harrier 150
    Hurricane 144
    Lancaster 90, 91
    Liberator 145
    Me-262 123
    Meteor 123
    MiG-15 124
    Mosquito 92
    Shooting Star 124
    Zero 150
Alam Halfa 71

188

Alamein 71
Alanbrooke, General 95, 167, 170
Albania 6, 39, 56
Albion 8
Alexander I, Tsar 116-7, 118
Alexander the Great 116
Alexandria 82, 119
Algeria 39, 52, 86-7
all arms 57, 68
alliance 1, 3, 11-12, 49
allies 1, 3-4, 13, 53, 114, 118, 167, 174
Allies, the (see also Anglo-)
  Britain/America 35, 36, 61, 62, 70, 71,
     78, 85-8, 91, 123, 157-8,
     160-1, 162, 164, 166,
     178, 182
  Britain/America/Russia 44, 46, 52, 174,
     179
  Britain/France 1, 21, 22, 27, 30, 36
Alte, die 78
Altmark 29-33
Altmayer, General 25
amateur 121-2, 125, 126, 127
America (inc US, USA) see also
           Anglo-American
  aces 77, 78
  air forces 78, 84, 86-7, 89-90, 92, 123,
     145, 170
  aircraft carriers 79-81
  allies 46, 85-6, 87-8, 97, 157-8, 162
  armies 19, 28, 47, 54, 82, 85, 127-9,
     141, 157-8, 162-3, 165,
     168, 170, 183
  anti- 99
  anti-communism 58
  anti-war 7, 8
  atomic bomb 49, 124, 170, 180, 182,
     184-6
  beltway 99
  bombing 85-8, 89-90, 92, 107, 170
  Britain 20, 39, 41-2, 46, 54, 69, 72,
     97, 122, 123-4, 128, 143,
     145, 146, 151, 157, 162,
     165, 168, 170, 172, 183,
     184, 185
  Cassino 84-6
  casualties 72, 89, 92, 135, 162-3, 171,
     183
  China 19, 42, 51, 185
  code-breaking 80
  colonial troops 3
  democracy 39, 41, 185-6
  Desert Storm 65, 113
  fleet 78, 80-1
  foreign policy 42-3, 97-100, 158,
     170-2

First World War 18, 20
France 20, 52
frit 72
garages 122
Germany 18, 20, 41, 54, 90-92, 97,
     123, 138, 171-2, 182
Great Depression 40, 41
Great Power 19, 43, 51, 52, 99-100,
     113, 115
guarantor power 8
industry 41, 123
invasions 39, 113, 145
Iran 44, 46-8, 49
island 1, 21, 158, 170, 185
isolationism 18, 40
Israel 65, 99-100, 105
Japan 18-19, 41, 58, 78-9, 107, 123,
     135, 149, 170-9, 172, 180,
     182-3, 184-6
Jews 97, 98, 99, 105
-ism 115
Korean War 77, 113, 123
marines 141, 170-1
material abundance 21, 42-3, 85, 172-3
media 123, 170
military diffidence 20-1, 128
navy 79-81, 137, 141, 144-5, 149, 151,
     170-2, 173
North Africa 35, 145, 157
North Korea 51, 116
pilots 77, 89
POWs 133-4
presidents 40, 42-3, 98-100, 170
Roosevelt (see main entry)
Russia 123, 181, 185-6
socialism 100
Spain 35
strongest army 19
submarines 78, 171
tanks 63, 65, 69-70, 72, 78, 141
troops 44, 46, 48, 49, 85, 87
Versailles 8, 43
Vietnam 58, 113
Americas 30, 41
Amiens 27-8
amphibious 55, 161
An American in Paris 172
Anglo-American
  armies 18, 35, 52, 71, 72, 85, 127,
     133, 157, 161, 163, 185
  atomic 180, 184
  Iran 46, 49
  Japan 183-5
  post-war 35, 49, 51-3, 186
  Russia 46, 182, 186
  strategic bombing 91

Anglo-Dutch wars 146, 147
Anglo-French 22, 31, 180
Anglo-German Naval Agreement 12
Anglo-Persian Oil Co 49
Angola 39
annexation 4, 9, 10, 45
Anschluss 4
anti-
  aircraft 75, 81, 162
  America 99
  British 47, 52, 53
  German 9, 20, 47, 52, 53, 54
  government 95
  Islamist 99
  Israel 99
  Russian 47
  Semitism 94, 97, 102
  shipping 142
  submarine 142, 143
  tank 67, 68, 75, 78, 165, 166
Antigua 41
Antwerp 141, 161
Anzio 33, 157-8
Appeasement 6, 18, 31-2
Arab 99, 105
Arbiter Power 8, 9, 12
archetype 94, 99
Ardennes 22, 23, 24
ardent spirits 128
Argentina 29, 30, 150
Arizona 90
armaments 9, 41, 59, 67, 89, 122, 174
armed forces /services)
  American 170-1, 185
  British 94, 126
  French 26
  German 176, 178
  Japanese 183
  Russian 174
  Yugoslav 57
  Turkish 36
Armenia 111
Armistice, the 51
armour (see also tank) 61, 63, 70, 74-5,
               147-8, 165
  Chobham 63
  column 71, 74, 75
  corps 166
  divisions 22, 23, 71, 74, 141, 164-5
  formation 166
  -piercing 67
  ships 147, 148
arms industry 10, 59-60, 92, 123, 178
army 23, 34, 64, 66, 71, 114, 116, 128,
        130, 133, 152-6, 159-60,
        165, 183

Allied 21, 22, 24, 70, 88
American 19, 28, 42, 47, 127, 128, 141,
        145, 158, 168, 169-71, 185
Air Force (USAAF) 170
Anglo-American 161
Belgian 24
British 2, 8, 20, 24, 28, 47, 48-9, 54,
        59, 74-5, 93-4, 95, 121,
        127, 128, 138, 143, 157-
        66, 167, 168, 169, 170
Canadian 161
Chinese 3, 173
Eighth 169
field 2, 21, 158, 184
French 18, 24, 25, 27, 28
German 13, 18, 23, 27, 36, 55, 65, 152,
        164-5, 168, 176-8, 179
Group North 59
Israeli 65
Italian 36
Japanese 16, 172-3, 184
Kitchener's 8
Kwantung 184
large(st) 3, 28, 158, 173, 179
private 127, 128
Russian (Red) 2, 3, 9, 32, 47, 59, 65,
        117, 132, 173, 184
strongest in world 19
tank 65, 70
Turkish 36
Vlasov 132
Yugoslavian 57
Arnhem 157-66
Arsenal of Democracy 41
artificial harbour 124
artillery 61-2, 64, 72, 73, 75, 85, 91
Ashkenazim 105
Asia 44, 173
Asquith, Herbert 167
atheist 98
Atlanta 63
Atlantic 54, 55, 119, 139, 140, 142, 143,
        144
  bases 41, 138
  Battle of 142, 143, 168
  North 135, 141, 152
  South 29
  Wall 125
atoll 172
atom 51, 154
  bomb 78, 124, 180, 181, 182, 184, 185,
        186
  secrets 124
  spies 124, 181
  war 19, 154

attack 51, 84, 140, 158-60, 163
air 81, 84, 140
American 52, 80-1, 157-8
British 38, 52, 148, 153, 157-8
counter- 73, 115
feint 22, 23, 160
German 22-4, 44, 73, 93, 115, 174-5
improvised 157
Japanese 80-81, 173, 175
kamikaze 81
main 160
river-crossing 158-60, 163
Russian 32, 115
spoiling 159
surprise 23, 24, 74, 163, 175
textbook 148
Attila the Hun 68
Auchinleck, General 128
Auschwitz 133
Australia 86, 106, 146
Austria 4, 5, 6, 10, 12, 103
autumn 91, 93, 115, 117, 164, 179
Axis, the 3
Balkans 36, 57, 118
Mediterranean 57, 72, 82, 119
Spain 34-5
ayatollah 49, 50
Aymes, General 25
Azerbaijan 45-46
Azores 39

B-17 89-90, 91-2
B-29 180
Bahamas 41
Balkans 4, 8, 36, 56-8, 118, 178
ball bearings 90
ballistic missile 180
balloon 21, 180
Baltic Sea 31, 59, 117, 118
Baltic States 32, 103
Bangladesh 111
banzai 80, 173
Barbarossa 117, 120
barrel
pickle 90
pork 170
rain 122
bases 41, 54, 138
battle 66, 72, 130, 156
air 78, 142
break-in 71
break-out 71, 72
British 70, 71, 85, 160
carrier 150-1
encirclement 60

-field 66, 67, 68, 69, 71, 72, 133, 135,
157, 167, 175
fleet 81, 82, 138, 149
Japanese 184
naval 80, 148, 150-1
plans 22
set-piece 74, 157, 160, 161
Whitehall 141-2, 151
see also individual battles
Alam Halfa 71
Alamein 71
Arnhem 157-66
Atlantic 143-4, 168
Borodino 115
Britain 77
Cambrai 64
Cannae 56
Cassino 85
Coral Sea 80
D-Day 87, 124, 161, 172
Dieppe 161
Jutland 137, 148, 149
Kiev 59, 60
Mareth Lines 71-2
Midway 80, 81
Moscow 175
Normandy 70, 72, 85
Pearl Harbour (see main entry)
River Plate 29
Schweinfurt 90
Stalingrad 119-20, 133
Taranto 149
Thermopylae 56
Tsushima 150
Villers-Bocage 74-6
battlecruiser 147-8
battleship 82, 135-6, 138, 147-8, 149-50
pocket- 29-30
Bayesian logic 78
bazooka 68
Belarus 102
Belgium
border 22, 164, 166
invaded 20-1, 22, 23, 24, 38, 55
neutral 38, 53, 55
surrender 24, 27
Belgrade 57
Belisha beacon 93
Beltway, the 99
Bendlerstrasse 179
Bentham, Jeremy 101
Berlin 32, 158
Berlin Decrees 117
Bessarabia 32
Bevan, Aneurin 95
Bevin, Ernie 153

191

biplane 150
Bismarck (ship) 148
Bismarck, Chancellor 96
Bletchley Park 125, 126
Blighty 132
Blitzkrieg 24, 27
blockade 31, 35, 41, 54
Blohm and Voss 153
blowback 127
bocage 75
Boche 61
boffin 152, 154
Bohemia 9, 10
Bolivia 39
bomb (–ing) (see also bomber) 86, 91
  America 81, 84, 86, 87, 88, 90, 91-2,
    170, 178, 182, 184, 185
  atomic 49, 124, 180-1, 182, 184, 185,
    186
  Britain 53, 56, 84, 86, 87, 88, 91-2, 107,
    141, 142-3, 169, 178
  bouncing- 121-2
  carpet 87
  Command 142, 143, 170
  conventional 182
  fire- 182
  -load 89, 92, 142
  Germany 54, 107
  Japan 41, 81, 107, 170
  precision 87, 89-90
  -sight 90, 123, 124
  strategic 53, 54, 92, 141, 170
  tactical 84
bomber 89, 91
  B-17 89-90, 91-2
  B-29 180
  dive 80-81
  Flying Fortress (see B-17)
  Halifax 90
  Harris 54, 90
  Lancaster 90-91
  Mosquito 92
  torpedo 80-81
  Wellington 122
books (etc) 84-5, 93, 94, 130, 160, 163,
    164, 175
border 17, 22, 108, 109, 174
  commission 108
  Dutch/German 126, 162, 164, 166
  French 6
  frontier 6, 21, 115
  incident 19
  Indian 111
  Italian 4
  Russo-German 32
  Russo-Iranian 45

Bore War 93
Borodino 115
bouncing bomb 121-2
bran tub 42
Brazil 39
Bren gun 10
Brest-Litovsk 117
bridge 157, 163
  Arnhem 158, 162, 163
  crossing 163
  golden 71, 72
  -head 163
Britain/British (see also Anglo-)
  aces 77, 78
  air force (RAF) 84, 86, 87, 89, 90, 92,
    123, 141-3, 150, 168, 169,
    170
  airborne 157-63
  America 18, 39, 41-2, 46-9, 52, 55, 65,
    69, 71, 72, 85, 87-8, 92,
    97-8, 99, 123-4, 126, 145,
    151, 157-8, 160-3, 165,
    185
  amateur 121-6
  appeasement 6-7, 13, 18
  army 2, 8, 10, 18, 20, 21, 24, 28, 36,
    47-9, 58, 59, 63, 74, 84,
    93-4, 95, 121, 125, 126,
    127, 128-9, 130, 133-4,
    154-5, 157-8, 160, 162,
    165, 166, 167, 168, 184
  blockade 30-1, 35, 41, 54, 137-8
  class 19, 94, 96-7, 121, 157, 165
  codes 57, 137
  colonial troops 3
  convoys 137-42, 144, 152-3
  Crete 56-7, 84, 85
  democracy 3, 5, 163, 185-6
  diplomacy 6-11, 32, 47-8, 93, 125
  dominions 7
  empire 2, 3, 44, 46, 74, 111, 121, 146,
    150, 168, 183
  ethnic cleansing 106, 110
  foreign policy 1-2, 5, 6-11, 13, 32-3,
    47-8, 53, 57-8, 97, 105,
    106
  France 1-2, 5, 6-12, 13, 20-1, 22, 24,
    27-8, 30-1, 52, 53, 61, 65,
    93, 114, 124
  frit 72
  generals 160, 169
  Germany 1, 5, 6, 11, 12, 13, 18, 20, 22,
    29-30, 32-3, 36, 51, 53-5,
    55, 56-7, 66, 74-5, 77, 84-
    5, 92, 97, 119, 123, 125-6,
    131-2, 136, 137-9, 148,

192

152-3
Great Power 5, 8, 9, 11, 12, 44, 52,
   114, 152
Greece 56 (and see Crete)
ground troops 84-5, 162
guarantor power 12
intelligence 123, 125
invasions 5, 33, 38-9, 45, 125
inventiveness 122-3, 124
Iran 44-50
island nation 1, 21, 158
Italy 5, 53, 56, 149
Japan 18, 147, 149, 150-1, 183
Jews 94, 96-7, 98-9, 105
Mediterranean 5, 34, 72, 82, 118-9, 168
Middle East 36, 38, 44, 57, 105, 118-9,
   168, 169
ministers 93-4, 96, 165, 168
navy 2, 29-30, 82, 116, 117, 119, 122,
   135-6, 137-8, 141-5, 146-
   7, 148-51, 168, 173
Normandy 62, 70, 72, 74-6, 87, 157
North Africa 35, 65, 71-2, 74, 76, 85,
   119, 157, 166
Norway 31-33, 38
operational research 152-3
perfidious 1, 8
planes 27, 141-5, 150
Poland 47
politics 93-6, 96-7, 98-9, 167
politic(king) 94-6, 126, 141-3, 167-8
POWs 30, 32, 130-32, 133-4
railways 45, 68-9
retreat 24, 38, 57, 62, 64, 76, 84, 87,
   166
Russia 1-2, 6, 36, 44-8, 58, 72, 114,
   117, 123-4, 185
snooker 48
Spain 5-6, 34, 35,
sphere of influence 44
spies 42, 124, 125-6, 127
sport 48, 77, 121, 131
strategic bombing 53, 90-91, 141, 170
strategic interests 32, 44-9, 118-9, 146
tanks 61, 62-3, 64, 65, 67, 68-72, 73-5,
   78, 141, 164-5
technology 89-90, 92, 123
trade 8, 117, 161
troops 3, 162, 164-5
Turkey 35-6, 118
war crime 132
Yugoslavia 57
Brno 10
Browning, General 165
Buenos Aires 30
build-up 159, 160, 161, 165

Bulgaria 34, 57
bulldozer 75
bureaucrat 174, 177
Burma 128, 168, 171, 173
Bushido 80
Butler, R.A. 107
Byelorussia 174
Byng, Admiral 173

C 63, 126
CAM 144
CIA 42
cabinet 46, 93, 94, 95, 168, 172
   committee 142
   government 95, 168, 169
   minister 96, 98
   papers 119
   rank 94
   War- 153, 182
Caen 87
Cambodia 39, 58
Cambrai 64
camp
   concentration 176
   gulag 133, 173
   labour 104
   summer 48
campaign 78, 154, 158, 165
   American 158, 161, 171
   Arnhem 157-66
   bombing 91
   British 54, 74, 84, 85, 87, 128, 146,
      149, 157-66, 168
   Burma 128, 168
   Canadian 161
   Crete 84
   French 116
   German 22, 24, 33, 54, 75, 116, 179
   Japanese 173, 184
   Normandy 74, 87
   Norwegian 33, 85
   Russian 149, 183, 185
   submarine 171
   Western Desert 75, 85
Canada 161-2
cancer 112
Cannae 56
capital
   city 11, 32, 59-60, 116, 126
   ship 82
carpet bombing 87
carrier (see aircraft carrier)
Cassino 85-6
casualties (inc deaths etc)
   American 72, 135, 162-3, 183, 184

British 30, 72, 136, 142-3, 162-3, 182, 184
  German 30, 133, 182
  Iranian 47
  Japanese 135, 180, 182-3
  neutrals 34
  Russian 133
caterpillar tracks 61
Catholic 98, 115
Caucasus 120
cavalry 66-7
Challenger II 62-3
Chamberlain, Neville 7, 25, 93, 95, 167
Channel 4 131
Char de bataille 61, 67
Chechens 105
Chequers 142
Chiang Kai-shek 3
Chiang Kai-shek, Madame 42
Chief of Staff 48, 142
Chile 39
China 16, 21, 39, 113, 173
  America 19, 42, 51, 58, 170-1, 185
  Japan 16, 19, 173, 183
Chindits 128
Chobham 63
Chorleywood 63
Christian 98, 99
Church of England 98
Churchill (tank) 62
Churchill, Winston
  appeasement 18
  empire 18, 41, 168
  enjoys war 178
  First Lord 32, 94, 168
  France 25, 95
  Hore-Belisha 93-6
  Iran 48
  prime minister 94-5, 126, 168
  Roosevelt 41, 42, 128, 170
  Stalin 58
  tanks 62, 71, 141
  Turkey 36
  war leader 71, 160, 167-9, 179
  writing 63, 93, 95, 160
civil service 176
Civil War
  American 40, 63
  Spanish 5-6, 34
civilian 48, 94, 107, 132, 167, 168, 173, 174, 182, 184-5
Clydeside, Red 91
co-belligerent 118
coal 11, 125
coast(line) 22, 28, 41, 115, 158, 161, 170-1

codes 57, 80, 126, 137
Cold War 99
collectivisation 106
Colombia 39
Colonel Blimp 122
colonial troops 3
command(ers)
  army 60, 71, 74, 93-4, 95, 163, 165, 166
  battlefield 93-4, 161, 167
  Bomber 142-3, 170
  centre 66
  chain of 172
  corps 25, 93-4, 95
  divided 141
  ground 87
  high 22, 86
  in chief 25-6, 93, 162, 169, 174, 178
  militia 108
  naval 29
  submarine 78
  tank 27, 74, 78
Commandos 128
commerce raiding 29
committee 63, 142, 155
Commons, House of 95
communiqué 128
communism 49, 57, 115, 175
  Cambodian 58
  Chinese 58
  Iranian 45-46, 50
  Russian 46, 175
  Vietnamese 58
  world 58
comrade 42, 154-5, 165
concentration
  artillery 85
  camp 176
  force 119, 120, 159
  ships 137
  tanks 27, 64
Confederates (US) 19
conference 14, 185
  Munich 12, 13
  Potsdam 49, 185
  Quebec 128
  Tehran 185
  Versailles 43
  Wannsee 120
  Yalta 182, 185
Congress 40, 80
conscription 127
Conservative (party) 91
conspiracy 49
  theory 123, 124
constitutional 169, 172, 177

194

Continental System 118
convoy 140, 152-3
  codes 137
  escorts 137, 139, 140
  planes 140-1, 142, 144
  submarines 137-8, 139, 140, 153
Coral Sea 80
cordon sanitaire 8, 9, 20
corps
  XXX 162, 163, 164, 165
  armoured 166
  commander 25, 93, 95
  Marine 141, 170
corvette 139, 140
counter-
  attack 74, 115
  claim 98
  measures 69, 153, 159
  moves 18
  offensive 159, 163
  perfidiousness 1
  productive 99
  stroke 143
coup 57, 94
Courageous HMS 144
court martial 136
Coventry 107
Crete 33, 56, 68, 84, 86
cricket 121
crime 105, 106, 131-2, 176
Crimean War 118
Croatia 57, 107-110
crossing the T 71
cruise missile 180
cruiser
  ship 29, 30, 138, 148
  tank 62
cryptanalysis 125
cryptography 125
Cuba 39
Cup, the 15, 19
Czechoslovakia 6, 9-14, 103

D-Day 87, 124, 161, 172
Daladier, Edouard 25
Dakar 52
Dam Busters 121-2
damage control 81, 82
Day of Infamy 172
day(time) 139, 140, 163, 165
De Gaulle, General 20, 26
deaths (see also casualties)
  American 92, 134, 171
  Anne Frank 107
  atomic 180, 182

  Australian 106
  British 106, 133, 136
  French 27
  German 106, 110, 132, 133, 180
  Indian 110-1
  Iranian 47
  Japanese 107, 171, 182
  Jewish 101, 104, 106, 107, 110, 111
  minorities 102, 106, 177
  neutrals 34
  Polish 105
  Roosevelt 43, 98, 100
  Russian 106, 132-3
  Rwandan 110
  Todt, Fritz 178
  Yugoslav 109
defence 51, 52, 68, 108-9, 162, 164,
  American 81
  fixed 20, 26, 55, 72, 86, 125, 159
  French 23, 24, 26, 55, 72
  German 86, 125, 157, 160, 161, 165
  Japanese 80
  prepared 23, 165, 174
  river crossings 158-60
  Russian 120
delivery system 51, 78
Democracies, the 4-5, 39, 163, 177
democracy 3-6, 41, 177
Denmark 38, 53, 55, 117
Depression, Great 40, 41
depth charge 142, 153
desert 47, 65, 84, 90, 128, 166
  Negev 105
  Rats 74, 75
  Western 65, 71, 74, 75
  Storm I, II 65
design(er) 21, 62, 67, 69, 89, 90, 122,
          139, 147, 174
destroyer 32, 41, 138, 169
Detroit 72
Devonshire, Duke of 167
dictator 3-6, 18, 34, 35, 40
Dieppe 161
diminishing marginal utility 104, 142
diplomacy 4, 6, 9, 42, 47-8, 93, 125, 175
  Nelsonian 32
Disraeli, Benjamin 98
divisions 1-2, 33, 119, 169
  armoured 22, 23, 64, 65, 68, 71, 141,
          165
  Hitler Youth 78
  infantry 24, 85
  motorised 23-4
  Seventh Armoured 74-5
doctrine 155, 159
  airborne 162

195

British 131, 135, 150
Monroe 41
tactical 74, 75
tank 64, 78
Dodecanese 33, 169
Dominican Republic 39
Dönitz, Admiral 78
Drang nach Osten 1
Dreadnought, HMS 147, 149
du Maurier, Daphne 165
Dutch (Holland) 38, 53, 55, 125, 146,
         147, 153, 158, 162, 164

88mm gun 75
east(ern) 21, 32, 60, 87, 114
Europe 102, 103
Far 17, 18, 58, 168, 175
Front 2, 22, 91, 133
Middle (see main entry)
East Germany 50
Ecole Spéciale Militaire 61
economy
American 170
German 54, 91, 175, 176-8, 180
British 91-2, 170
slumps 40, 41, 176
warfare 125, 127
Eden, Anthony 48
efficiency
German 57, 62, 176, 177-8
least 180
most 180-1
Peter Principle 154
ego 116
Egypt 36, 39, 54, 57, 65, 118, 119
Eighth Army 169
Eisenhower, General 162, 174
El Alamein 71
El Salvador 39
election 98, 99, 108, 169, 171-2, 185-6
Elephant (tank) 62
empire/emperor
Austro-Hungarian 10
British 2, 46, 74, 121, 146, 150, 168,
         183
German 179
Japanese 136, 150, 184
en masse (tanks) 64-72
Enfield 10
England (see Britain)
English Channel 21, 22, 28, 124
Episcopalian 98
escort 133
plane 81
ship 41, 137, 138, 139, 140

espionage 181 (see also intelligence,
         spies)
esprit de corps 84
Estonia 102
Ethiopia (Abyssinia) 5, 6
ethnic cleansing 104, 106, 107, 109, 111
ethnicity 99
Etna Principle 102
eugenics 102
Europe
America 8, 18, 90, 161, 170, 172
anti-Semitism 102-3, 120
arbiter of 8
blockade of 54
holocausts 111
ills of 107
largest country 9
last fascist regime 35
neutrals 7, 117
peace in 8, 54
powers 11, 13, 114
secret services 125, 127
Sick Man of 8
subjugation 113-4, 116
war in 30, 72
exile 53, 105, 174
experiment 65, 85, 90, 106, 123, 177,
         186
explosive 67, 148, 180

facts on the ground 108, 109
Falklands 150, 165
famine 106
fanaticism 136
Far East 18, 175
fascism 25, 35, 46
fatherland 29
Federals (US) 19
feint 22, 23, 160
felicific calculus 101, 103, 104, 107
Fifth Republic 20
fighters (see airplanes)
film (see also newsreels) 121-2, 130,
         157, 163, 164
Finland 3, 17, 30, 31, 32, 59, 117
fire (-ing)
anti-aircraft 81
-fight 82-3
line 24, 69
squad 131-2
-storm 107, 182
submarine 138-9
Firefly (tank) 63
First Amendment 133
First Lord 32

First Sea Lord 94, 168
First World War (inc Great War etc)
  aces 77
  America 18, 20, 71
  aviation 89, 92, 141
  Britain 18, 20, 64-5, 71, 92, 94, 96,
      137, 138, 141, 144, 147
  France 18, 20, 22, 24, 26, 27, 28, 64-5,
      77
  Germany 3-4, 18, 20, 22, 24, 26, 28,
          30-1, 33, 38, 113, 117,
          137, 138, 175, 178, 184
  neutrals 22, 24, 34, 38
  Russia 18, 20, 33, 117, 123, 175
  ships 41, 137, 138, 144, 147
  tanks 64-5, 71, 141
Fisk, Robert 111
fixed defences 20-21, 24
fjord 30, 148
flak (see also anti-aircraft) 92, 162
flat-tops 144
fleet (see also navies for each
          country)
  Air Arm 141, 144
  American 78, 80-81, 146
  battle 81, 82, 138, 149, 151
  British 82, 116, 147, 148, 149, 151
  German 137, 138, 149
  in being 82
  Italian 82
  Japanese 78, 80-81, 150
  merchant 139
  Russian 149, 150
Flying Fortress (B-17) 89-90, 91-2
Focke-Wulf 144
food (etc) 30, 35, 47, 106, 168, 171
football 15
following orders 132
force(s) (see also armed, air etc)
  Allied 31, 36, 49, 157, 167, 173
  American 81
  British 48, 74, 179
  build-up of 159
  concentration of 119, 120
  French 22, 23, 26, 119
  German 59, 71, 87, 164
  ground 84
  Italian 71
  Japan 173, 183
  majeure 31
  minimum 173
  multiplier 20
  overwhelming 135, 157, 159, 173
  reconnaissance in 74
  Russian 1, 47, 120, 175
  special 128

foreign
  Office 47, 48, 168
  policy 3, 20, 42, 52-3, 58, 97, 100, 116,
      158, 185-6
  Secretary 48, 165
form guide 15-19
Four Year Plan 177
fox 26, 29
France (see also Anglo-French)
  aces 77
  Africa 5, 38, 87, 118
  appeasement 7
  arbiter power 8-9, 11-12
  army 3, 22, 24, 25-8
  Britain (and USA) 1, 2, 4-5, 9-13, 22,
      27-8, 30-1, 33, 38, 52-5,
      61, 65, 93, 95, 117, 124,
      143
  Czechoslovakia 9-13
  eastern possessions 18, 26, 58, 118
  Fall of 26-8, 41, 121, 138
  foreign policy 9, 20, 52-3
  Franco-Prussian War 23
  Free 72, 86, 85
  Germany 9-13, 18, 20-21, 23-4, 28, 30,
      41, 51-3, 118, 138
  government 25-6
  occupation 18, 118
  Poland 6, 9-13
  Resistance 127
  Russia 6, 20, 33, 113-4, 117, 118
  tanks 27, 61, 65, 67, 68
Franco, Francisco 5, 6, 34-5, 36
Frank, Anne 107
frit 72
front 20, 24, 68, 141, 174
  air 169
  Atlantic 55
  Eastern 2, 22, 91, 133
  fighting 85, 169
  home 77
  -line 18, 59, 83, 95, 161
  linear 158-9
  southern 119
  united 12
  Western 2, 30
frontier (see also borders) 6, 21, 115,
      174
Fuchs, Klaus 124
fuel 124, 142
Führer 34 (also see Hitler)
Führerprinzip 176-9
funnies (tanks) 124
furniture 92

GCHQ 137
G.I's 133
Galicia 10
Gamelin, General 25, 26
garage 27, 122
garden shed 122
garrison 56, 86, 135, 171
general(s) 22, 71, 115, 128, 157, 158,
        160, 164
    American 63, 128, 157
    British 128, 157, 160, 168-9
    French 25-6
    German 14, 22, 164, 178
    Russian 174
    also see individual generals
    Alanbrooke 95, 167, 170
    Altmayer 25
    Auchinleck 128
    Aymes 25
    Browning 165
    de Gaulle 20, 26
    Eisenhower 161-2, 174
    Gamelin 25, 26
    Giraud 25
    Gort 93, 95
    Grant 160
    Huntziger 25
    Ludendorff 60
    MacArthur 86, 170, 171
    Manstein 22-4, 27
    Marshall 97, 170
    McClellan 171
    Model 163-4
    Moltke 60
    Montgomery (see main entry)
    Patton 88
    Pownall 95
    Stillwell 128
    Weygand 26
    Wingate 128
General Secretary 2
General Staff 22, 23, 60, 152, 179, 184
General Winter 115
genes 101-2
genius 167, 178, 180
genocide 110, 111
geopolitics 48
George VI 94
Germany
    aces 77, 78, 79
    air (-planes. Luftwaffe etc) 77, 85, 89,
        90, 91-2, 142, 144, 149,
        177, 180
    America 18, 20, 41, 52, 54-5, 77, 85-8,
        89-90, 91, 97, 157, 160-1,
        162-5, 171-2

anti- 9, 20, 47, 52, 52-4, 77, 78
army 13, 18, 20-1, 23-4, 27, 28, 36, 55,
        59-60, 68, 85-6, 152, 157,
        160-6, 169, 178
Austria 4-5, 6, 12
Balkans 33, 36, 38, 56-7, 118, 169, 178
Belgium 22-4, 38, 51-2
Britain 1, 5, 6, 12, 13, 18, 20, 22, 24,
        29-33, 51-5, 56-7, 66, 71,
        74-5, 77, 85-8, 91-2, 93,
        106, 119, 122, 125-6, 131-
        2, 137-8, 142-3, 148-9,
        157, 160-1, 162-6, 169
Czechoslovakia 9-10, 13, 104
defeat of 26, 30, 47, 48, 151, 178, 179,
        182, 184
East 50
economy (etc) 31, 32, 36, 54, 56-7, 90-
        91, 97, 119-20, 126, 176-8,
        180
First World War 18, 20, 22, 24, 26, 28,
        30, 33, 38, 64, 113, 117,
        146, 147, 175, 184
foreign relations 6, 13, 17-18, 20, 32-3,
        34, 36, 44-5, 51- 5, 116,
        118-20
France 5, 6, 8-13, 18, 20-1, 22-4, 26-8,
        30-1, 41, 51-3, 66, 118,
        152
Good 29
Greece 56-7, 139
guns 29, 61-2, 70, 75, 78, 87, 92, 147,
        162, 166
invasion(s) 6, 12, 20, 22-4, 33, 38, 53-
        4, 57, 113-4
Italy 1, 3-6, 33, 36, 41, 53, 118, 178
Japan 1
Jews 96, 102-4, 110, 120
Mediterranean 118-9, 168
Nationalists 4
navy 29-30, 123, 135-6, 137, 138, 146,
        147, 148-9
North Africa 36, 65, 71, 85, 118, 178
Norway 30-3, 38, 51-2, 139, 178
occupation 18, 118
Poland 6, 9, 12-13, 47, 66, 102-4
POWs 131-3
radar 122-3
Russia 1, 6, 18, 19, 32-3, 44-5, 47, 55,
        59-60, 65, 113-6, 117-8,
        119-20, 132-3, 174-5, 179
Sick Man 8, 12
Spain 5-6, 34-5, 118
-speaking 4, 9, 13, 104, 156, 180-1
submarines 41, 78, 137, 138-40, 142,
        144-5, 153

198

superiority 21, 24, 102, 152, 157, 169
tanks 23, 60, 61-2, 63, 64-5, 66, 68, 70, 71, 74-5, 78, 164-5
troops 23, 33, 53, 57, 72, 85-6, 87, 118, 119, 152, 169, 178-9
Turkey 35-6, 118-9
unification 20
Weimar 8, 65, 96
West 97
Yugoslavia 33, 38, 57
Ghazni Jail 134
Gibraltar 6, 34, 35, 118, 119
Giraud, General 25
Glasgow 91
glider 162, 180
global (*see* world)
Glorious HMS 148
Gloster Meteor 123
Gneisenau 135
Goebbels, Joseph 96, 98
Goering, Herman 177-8
golden bridges 71-2
Goldwater, Barry 98
Good German 29
Good Soldier Schweik 9
Gort, General 93, 95
Goumiers 86-7
government 64, 108, 110, 111, 167, 173
American 169, 172
Australian 85
British 94-5, 96, 98, 122-3, 132, 168, 172
Canadian 161
Chinese 16
exiled 53
French 25, 26
German 64-5, 96, 176-8
Iranian 45-47, 49
Israeli 127
Japanese 172-3, 184
legitimate 6
revolutionary 64-5
Russian 59, 174
Turkish 36
Graf Spee 29-30, 123
Grand Coalition 95
Grand Strategy 29, 30, 32, 33, 42, 119, 168, 171, 173, 174, 178
Grande Armée 114
Grant, General 160
Grant (tank) 67
Great Depression 40
Great Dictators, the 3-7
Great Escape 131
Great Escape 130
Great Game 44, 45

Great Patriotic War 19
Great Power 6, 8, 9, 15-16, 19, 20, 36, 51, 52, 54, 79, 100, 113, 116, 117, 152, 178
America 18-19, 20, 50, 52, 79-80, 99-100
Britain 20, 34, 50, 52, 114, 152
China 16
France 52, 116, 152
Germany 4, 17, 34, 116, 152, 178
Italy 4
Japan 79-80
neutrals and 31, 35, 36
Russia 19, 114
system 4, 8, 11, 12-13, 52, 114
Great War (see First World War)
Greece 33, 34, 39, 56-58, 139
Grenada 39
Grimsbottom Rovers 15
grip 168, 169
ground forces 84-8
Guarantor Power 12
Guatemala 39
Guilty Men 6
gulag 133, 173
Gulf, the 146
Gulf War I, II 113
Guyana 39
gun 69, 71, 72, 84, 87, 135, 147, 150
3.7 inch 75
6, 8-inch 29, 148
11, 12-inch 29, 147
14, 15-inch 74, 147
18-inch 147, 149
37, 50 mm 75
75 mm 27, 75
88 mm 75
17-pounder 63, 70
anti-aircraft (flak) 75, 92, 162
anti-tank 67-8, 75, 166
armour-piercing 67
Bren 10
deck 138
high explosive 67
-line 68, 71, 75
machine 62, 77, 89, 90
self-propelled 61-2, 78
-ships 68

Habsburg 8, 118
Haiti 39
Halifax (bomber) 90
Hamburg 55, 107, 126
harbour (see also port) 82, 123, 124, 149

Harrier 150
Harris, Air Marshal 54, 90
Harwood, Commodore 29
helicopter gunship 68
Heligoland Bight 54, 55
Hell's Highway 166
helmet 84, 88, 134
hero 9, 25, 43, 164
Hindu 111
Hiroshima 170, 182, 185, 186
historians
  Churchill as 71, 95, 160
  Churchill by 93, 168
  criticise Montgomery 71, 160
  disregard Phoney War 93
  feebleness of 20
  judge by association 40
  misinterpret campaigns 115
  quandary of 26
  revisionist 167
history
  books 93, 94, 130, 131, 160, 163, 164,
              175, 184
  cannot be rerun 59
  curse of 146
  human 6, 102, 184
  recent 94, 97, 111
  recorded 19
  tales of 6
  world (record) 19, 42, 122, 165
  written by winners 25
Hitler, Adolf
  accession 4, 5, 11, 12
  administrator 131-2, 175-8
  ego 116
  foreign policy 4, 12, 36
  Franco 34-5
  ideology 3, 115-6, 176
  intellectual 4
  Jews 120
  military leader 13-14, 22-4, 30, 39, 59-
              60, 70-71, 138, 164, 178-9
  Mussolini 3-5
  Napoleon 113-120
  Stalin 32, 116, 118
  strategist 17-18, 32-3, 51-5, 56-7, 119,
              139, 178
Hitler Youth Division 78
Ho Chi Minh 58
Holland 38, 53, 55, 125, 146,147, 153,
              158, 162, 164
Hollywood 89
holocaust 101, 105-6, 110-11, 132
Holocaust, The 101, 103, 111
  deniers 106
home front 77

Home Islands (Japan) 183, 184
homeland 34
Honduras 39
honour 80, 128, 136
Hood HMS 148
Hopkins, Harry 42
Hore-Belisha, Leslie 93-5, 96
horse 23, 25, 107
House of Commons 95
Howard, Michael 98
Hungary 10, 103
Huntziger, General 25
Hutus 110
hypocrisy 5, 101

Iceland 39
ichi 185
ideology 1, 3, 5, 35, 99, 106, 116
Inchon 55
independence
  France 52, 53
  Iran 44, 50
  neutrals 53
Independent, The 111
India 44, 111
Indian Ocean 44, 119, 146
Indo-China 18
Indonesia 39, 173
industry 11, 41, 59, 92, 97, 177-8
  aerospace 176
  arms 9
  -military complex 123
  oil 49
infantry 64, 65, 66, 85, 86,
  British 71, 72, 74, 85, 141, 169
  French 27
  German 22, 23, 24, 85
influence 4, 44, 96
infrastructure 131, 163
innovation 180
insurrection 31, 45-6
intellectual 4, 152
intelligence 123, 125, 174-5
intelligent 152-6
intelligentsia 152
interests, national 1, 6, 32, 37, 72, 97,
              116, 146
interwar years 64, 137, 138
invasion 5, 53, 54, 113, 172
  Albania 6, 39, 56,
  Algeria 39, 145
  Austria 4, 6, 12
  Belgium 20, 38, 55
  Britain 115, 168
  China 16, 39

200

Denmark 38, 55
Ethiopia 5
Gibraltar 34
Greece 39, 56
Holland 38, 55
Iran 38, 39, 45
Japan 171, 183
Korea 39, 113
Lebanon 38, 39
Luxembourg 38
Madagascar 38
Manchuria 16
Morocco 39, 145
Norway 31, 33, 38, 93
Portugal 39
Russia 113, 114, 117, 169, 174
South Korea 51
Spain 35, 36
Sweden 31, 38
Syria 38, 39
Tunisia 39, 145
Turkey 35, 36
Yugoslavia 38, 39
invention 122, 124
   American 69, 180
   British 63, 69, 101, 122, 123, 124, 141
   Dutch 153
   German 123, 180
   Japanese 180
   Russian 181
Inverness 115
Iran 38, 39, 44-50, 120
Iraq 38, 39, 44, 66, 120
Ireland 37, 77, 106
Irgun 127
Iron Cross 78
iron ore 31, 32, 38
irregulars 58
Isaacs, Rufus 96
ISIS 84
Islam (also Muslim) 50, 99, 115, 170,
island 30, 80, 135, 158, 173
   hopping 171
   Japanese 171, 183, 184
   nations 1
   Pacific 80, 135, 173, 185
isolationism 18, 40
Israel 65, 99-100
Italy 1, 34, 39, 82
   Abyssinia 5, 6
   Balkans 4, 6, 8, 56, 57
   Britain 4-5, 53, 56, 66, 71, 82, 147, 149
   Ethiopia 5, 6
   France 4-5, 8, 11, 53, 72
   Germany 1, 3-6, 33, 36, 41, 53, 71, 118,
         178

Mediterranean 4, 8, 53, 82, 118, 149
Versailles 4, 8

Jamaica 41
Japan 1, 16-17, 18, 19, 48, 80, 130, 172,
         173, 175, 182-3, 185
   aces 78-9, 81, 82
   America 18-19, 41, 58, 78, 79-81, 107,
         123, 128, 130, 135, 149,
         170-1, 172, 180, 182-3,
         184-6
   Britain 2, 18, 48, 128, 146-7, 149-51,
         168, 183, 184
   casualties 135, 182-3, 186
   China 16-17, 19, 173, 183
   government 172-3, 182
   kamikaze 81, 82
   navy 79-81, 123, 147, 149-51, 172, 173
   planes 77, 150
   Roosevelt 41, 123, 128, 171-2
   Russia 17, 19, 47, 150, 175, 182, 183-7
   soldiers 21, 130, 135, 136, 172, 184
   surrender 47, 130, 182, 183, 185, 186
   technology 21, 78-9, 180
jaw-jaw 63
Jazz Age 11
jeep 77, 145
Jellicoe, Admiral 137
jets 123, 150
Jew(ish)
   America 97-100, 105
   archetype 94, 99
   Ashkenazim 105
   diaspora 105
   Eastern Europe 102-3
   Germany 96, 102, 106, 107, 110, 120
   Israel 65, 99-100, 105
   killing of 101, 103-4, 106, 107, 110,
         111
   lobby 99
   office, in 94, 96-100, 127
   Poland 102-4, 105
   relocation 103-5
   wartime, in 96, 97
   Zionists 120
July Plot 178
Jutland 137, 148, 149

Kaiser 178
kamikaze 81, 151
Kashmir 111
Katyn 105
Keynes, Maynard 176
Khomeini, Ayatollah 49

kibbutz 105
Kiev 59, 60
Kim Jong-un 51, 116
Kitchener's Army 8
Korea 39, 51, 55, 113, 135, 185
Korean War 77, 113, 123
Kremlin 174
Kriegsmarine 30, 78, 138
kulaks 106
Kuriles 185
Kwantung Army 183

labour 121, 133
  camp 104
Lancaster 90, 91
landing 35, 57, 74, 157, 161
  craft 172
  take-off and 144
  zone 162
Langsdorff, Captain 29-30
Laos 39
Latvia 102
law/legality 29, 48, 176
Leader of the Opposition 95
Leads, The 30, 31, 33
League of Nations 9, 11
leagues, football 15, 17
Leavenworth 174
Lebanon 38, 39, 52, 118
Lebensraum 118
left-wing 26, 95, 100, 115
Lenin, V.I. 113, 175
Leningrad 59-60
liberal 99
Liberal (party) 95
Liberation, the 51-52
Liberator (airplane) 145
Liberia 39
Libya 33, 36, 39, 56
Lincoln, President 40, 171
line
  defence 48, 74, 160
  firing 24, 69
  front 18, 22, 59, 83, 95, 159, 161
  gun 68, 71, 75
  integrity of 76
  killing 106
  Maginot 20-1
  Mareth 71-2
  production 70
  start 64, 66, 76, 87
  supply 46
Lithuania 102
Little Entente 9, 11, 12, 13
littoral (see also coast) 119

Liverpool 153
Lloyd George, David 167
logistics 46, 48, 133, 151, 158
London 32, 78, 169
long range 180
  Desert Group 128
  plane 142, 144
Lord, Thomas 121
Lord's cricket ground 121
losses (see casualties)
Low Countries 164
Ludendorff, General 60
Luftwaffe (see also air forces, German
      air-)
  Britain 54, 89, 91, 119, 123
  development 123, 177-8
  naval aircraft 149
  premier air force 89
  strategic bombing 91
Luxembourg 38, 53

M 126
MEW 126, 127
MI6 125, 126, 127
MiG-15 124
MacArthur, General 86, 169, 171
machine gun 62, 77, 89, 90
Madagascar 38, 52, 104, 105
Maginot Line 20, 26
majority 10, 102, 107-8
Malaya 146, 173
Malta 119
Manchester United 15, 16
Manchuria 16, 183, 185
manoeuvres 64, 67, 69, 72, 87, 116, 140
Manstein, General 22-24
Manstein Plan 22-24, 27
March on Rome 3
Mareth Lines 72
marines 2, 141, 170, 171
Market Garden 157-66
Marshall, General 170
Marshall Plan 97
Marxism 115 (also see communism)
mass production 69, 78
matériel 21, 184
Matilda (tank) 75
McClellan, General 171
mechanismo 86
media (see newspapers, books etc)
Mediterranean
  Britain 34, 72, 118, 168
  Germany 34, 118-9
  Italy 4-5, 8, 53, 82, 149
Meiji Restoration 19

202

Memel 6
Merchant Navy 29, 138, 143
Merrill's Marauders 128
Mers-el-Kébir 52
Messerschmitt Me-262 123
Meuse 23
Middle East 36, 119, 120, 168, 169
Midway 80, 81, 150
Milch, Erhard 177
Miliband, Ed 98, 99
military 6, 12, 21, 31, 130, 155, 156,
    159,   167, 184
  Allied 36
  America 90, 97, 123, 158
  Britain 49, 84, 95, 114, 121, 142, 152-
    3, 158
  coup 94
  doctrine 64, 74-5, 78, 135, 150, 155,
    159, 162
  failures 114, 121, 179
  forces 1, 36
  France 53, 61, 113-4
  Germany 33, 54, 97, 113-4, 132, 178-9,
    180
  government 156, 173
  hardware 69, 78
  historians 20, 26, 71, 93, 115, 160, 166
  -industrial complex 123-4
  Italy 4, 53, 82
  Japan 173, 183-4
  Russia 1, 114, 123, 174
militia 108-10
mines 38, 68
minister/ministry
  Admiralty (see main entry)
  Air 122
  cabinet 96, 98
  communist 46
  Defence 168
  Economic Warfare 126-7
  Exchequer 168
  Food 168
  Foreign 47, 48, 125-6, 168
  Japanese 185
  Jewish 96-7, 98
  Navy (US) 169
  prime 93, 94, 126, 142, 168, 172
  service 168
  State (US) 47
  Supply 168
  Treasury (US) 97-8
  War 48, 93, 94, 96
minorities 9, 13, 101, 102
missile 68, 78, 180
Model, General 163, 164
modern(ise) 23, 25, 26, 27, 36, 41, 63,

    65, 71, 77, 82-3, 94, 106,
    152
Molotov-Ribbentrop Pact 6, 18, 32, 116
Moltke, General 60
monarch 169, 172
Mongols 19, 117
Monroe Doctrine 41
Montagu, Edwin 96
Monte Cassino 86
Montevideo 29, 123
Montgomery, General 71-2, 74, 87, 160,
    161
moral 58, 110, 113
morale 30, 78, 92, 113
Morgenthau, Henry 97-8, 99
Morgenthau Plan 97-8
Mormon 98
Morocco 34, 39
Moscow 45, 59-60, 115, 116, 175
Moseley, Oswald 107
Mosquito 92
motherland 133
mouseholing 86
Mulberry (harbour) 124
mud 115, 165
mum 60, 130
Munich Conference 12-13
Munich Putsch 3
murder 106
  judicial 132
  mass 106
Murmansk 2
Muslim (see also Islam) 111
Mussolini, Benito 3, 4, 5, 6
myth 164

NATO 35, 117
NCO 127
NKVD 47, 106
NSA 42
Nagasaki 170, 182, 185, 186
Napoleon 8, 113-9
Napoleon III 8, 118
Narvik 38
nation(al)
  at war 63, 78, 82, 123, 130, 146, 173,
    184
  character 11, 21, 80, 82, 85, 176, 184
  hero 9, 135, 164
  interest 1, 37, 96, 116
  island 1
  -ism 4, 11, 49, 50
  liberated 53
  most favoured 51, 54
  new 9, 107, 109

small 38
navy 68, 71, 148, 173
  American 41, 42, 80-81, 137, 141, 143,
         145, 146, 149, 151, 158,
         169-70, 171, 172, 173,
         184
  British 2, 12, 29-33, 35, 41, 74, 119,
         123, 135-6, 137-145, 146,
         148-51, 158, 173, 184
  German 12, 29-30, 78, 135-6, 137-8,
         142, 144, 146, 147, 148-9,
         177
  Italian 82, 149
  Japanese 80-81, 149-51, 151, 172-3
  merchant 29, 138
  Russian 174
Nazi 4, 101-2, 106, 107, 177
  -fied 78, 164
  holocaust 101, 107
  Party 176, 178
Nazi-Soviet Pact 6 (see also
        Molotov)
Negev Desert 105
negotiations 1, 10, 116
neighbour 12, 108, 109, 170
Nelson, Admiral 32
neuroses 11, 102
neutral
  America 35, 39, 123
  Belgium 24, 38, 53, 55
  capitals 32, 126
  First World War 34, 35, 38
  in war 31, 35, 55
  invasions 38-9, 53, 55
  maritime 29, 30, 31, 38
  Norway 30-2, 38, 53
  opinion 7, 30, 32
  Spain 35, 118
  Sweden 31, 37
  Turkey 34, 35-6
New Guinea 171
New Hampshire 99
New York 99
New Zealand 85-6
Newfoundland 41, 153
news(papers) etc
  American 123, 163, 170, 171
  Britain 121, 163
  contemporary 88, 99, 109, 134
  intelligence source 123, 125
  Independent 111
  German 78, 98
  Iranian 46
  media storm 29
  morale 128
  Newsnight 99

  -reels 3, 87, 171
  Russian (TASS) 186
Nicaragua 39
night(-time) 139, 163, 168
Nijmegen 165
Nippon (see also Japan) 18
Nobel Prize 95
non-aggression pact 17
Norden bombsight 90, 123, 124
Normandy 55, 62, 70, 72, 74, 75, 85, 87,
        157, 161
North
  Africa 35, 65, 85, 118, 145, 157, 178
  Atlantic 135, 140, 152
  Korea 39, 51, 55
  Sea 30, 31
  Vietnam 39
Norway
  Altmark 30, 32
  Finnish expedition 31
  invaded 32-3, 38, 93, 139
  neutral 53
  German bases 54, 148
  saboteurs 130
  troops in 33, 85, 178
nuclear 185 (see also atomic)
Nunn May, Alan 124
Nuremberg Trials 132
nutjob 98, 100

O-Group 155
OKH 179
OKW 179
OSS 128
observation post 86
occupation
  American 183
  British 38
  French 116, 117
  German 18, 36, 38, 59, 68, 117, 118,
        139
  Japanese 18, 171
  Russian 32
Ocean 21, 116, 124, 146, 150
  see also main entries
  Atlantic
  Indian
  Pacific
offensive
  American 157, 164
  British 72, 76, 157, 164
  counter- 159, 163
  German 25, 27-8, 163
officers
  American 127

204

British 29, 48, 125, 127, 131, 154-5, 157
Japanese 16
Polish 105
POW 130, 131
Staff college 152
Ohain, Hans von 123
oik 166
oil
  industry 44, 49, 126
  petrol 27, 67, 124
  pipeline 124
  supplies 32, 44-5, 48, 56, 119-20
  tankers 124, 144
Old Polish 10
Oman 62
One Navy Rule 146
open country 85, 87
Operational Research 152, 153
Oregon 180
orthodox 22, 24, 64
Oslo 32
Ost formations 133
Ottoman 8
over the top 87, 128
overflying 53-54
overwhelming (force) 66, 85, 109, 157, 159, 173

P & O 135
PLUTO 124
POW (see prisoners)
Pacific
  Ocean 135, 145, 146, 169, 180, 185
  War 78, 86, 169-70, 183, 185
pacifism 26
Packard truck 46
pact 17, 32 (see also Molotov)
Pakistan 39, 111
Palestine 118, 119, 120
Palmerston, Lord 167
panacea targets 90
Panama 39
panjandrum 90
Panther 62, 70
Panzer (see tank) (also see armoured)
Papacy 9, 86
parachute 144, 162, 163, 164
Paraguay 39
paratrooper 85, 86, 87, 162, 163, 166
Paris 24, 32, 93
partisan 127
partition 10-11, 110-11
party (political) 36, 45, 49, 50, 95, 99, 176, 178

Passport Control Officer 125, 126
patrol 30, 135, 140, 142-3, 159
Patton, General 88
peace
  conference 14, 185
  Europe 8, 54
  -loving democracies 39
  Serbs/Croats 107-8, 109
  settlement 13, 31, 51, 116, 123
  military in 125, 127, 154-5, 167
  suing for 16, 24, 183, 184
  talks 183, 186
  -time 96, 131
Peacock Throne 45
Pearl Harbour 41, 80, 82, 123, 149, 170
Peloponnese 56
peninsula 158
penny packets 64-72
perfidious 1, 8
perimeter 70, 74
Persian Gulf 45, 146
Peru 39
Pétain, Marshal 26
Peter Principle 154-5
petrol (see also oil) 27, 67, 124
phalanx 68
Philippines 39, 170-1, 173
Phoney War 93
photography 123
pilot 77, 78-9, 81-2, 180-1, 144, 150, 151, 177
pipeline 124
Pitt, William 167
plan(ning)
  American 35, 42, 47, 55, 85, 87, 165-6, 170
  British 2, 31, 35, 47, 55, 85, 87, 126, 149, 165-6
  French 20, 31
  German 17-18, 22, 30, 57, 65, 177
  Hitler 24
  Japanese 173
  Manstein 22-4, 27
  Marshall 97
  Morgenthau 97-8
  Schlieffen 24, 27
  Russian 65
  tanks 61, 65
plane (see airplane)
Plate, River 29, 30
Ploesti 32
pocket battleship 29-30
Poland 6, 9-14, 93
  Czechoslovakia 9-14
  France 6, 9, 11-13, 114-5, 119
  Germany 11-13, 32, 47, 66, 125

Jews 102-3, 105
Russia 9, 17, 32, 47, 106, 114-5, 119,
   174, 175
polderland 165
police
   intelligent 156
   secret 49-50
   -state 49, 156
   World- 8
politics
   American 98-100, 171-2
   British 93-4, 98, 168-9
   extreme 115-6
   German 177
   Great Power 9, 48
   Iranian 45
   occupation 47
politicking 126, 137, 155
Poltava 19
Pontecorvo, Bruno 124
Pope 9, 86
Porsche, Ferdinand 62
Port Arthur 149
ports 38, 44, 68-9, 161 (see also
   harbours)
Portugal 39
Potsdam Conference 49, 185
Pound, Admiral 168-9
powers (see also Great Powers) 9, 11, 12,
   31, 41, 97
   contiguous 17-18
   dominant 13, 113, 114, 117
   Far Eastern 18
   maritime 127, 158, 184
   medium 6
   small 34
   Western 174
Pownall, General 95
precision bombing 89-90
president 40, 98, 99
   Jewish 98, 99
   Lincoln 40, 171
   nut jobs 98, 100
   Roosevelt, F (see main entry)
   Roosevelt, T 40
   Truman 43
   Trump 116
   vice- 100
   Washington 40
   Wilson 8, 35, 43
press release 170
Prince of Wales, HMS 148
prisoners of war 30, 130-34
   books 130
   films 130
private army 127, 128

production 21, 42, 69, 70, 78, 91-2
professional 43, 121-8, 168, 170, 174,
   179
projective identification 116
promotion 155, 163
propaganda 96, 98, 106
protectorate 32, 119
prototype 144
Prussia 62, 117
psephology 177
psychopath 156
public relations 86, 170
Puerto Rico 39
Pyrenees 34

Quebec 128
Queen Elizabeth, HMS 82

RAF (see British air-)
race 9
racism 102, 110
radar 122-3
radio (wireless) 25, 27, 46, 137
raid 29, 90, 134, 170
railways 10, 16, 45, 46, 47, 48, 68-9,
   131, 164
Raj, the 146
Rangers 128
rank 128, 130, 155
Rank, Lord 122
Rapture, The 100
Raqqa 88
rasputitsa 115
Rawalpindi HMS 135-6
reconnaissance
   aerial 90, 144, 165
   in force 74
records 17, 77, 126, 182
Red
   Army (see Russia, armed forces)
   Clydeside 91
   Cross 130
Redford, Robert 165
redoubt 86, 125
refugee 27, 110
regulars 58, 127, 128
regime
   Ancien 65
   revolutionary 65
Reich 4, 177
reinforcements 74, 168
relocation 104, 105
republic 25
reputation 89, 126, 161, 162

206

reserve 23, 159
reservist 20
resign 172, 173 (see also sacking)
resistance 58, 127
resources 91, 119, 132, 167, 172, 177, 178
rest and recreation 165
retreat 62, 115, 166
revanchism 9
reverse slope 67
revolt 44
revolutionary 5, 59, 65
Reynaud, Paul 25-6
Rhine 23, 158, 161, 162, 163, 165-6
Rhineland 12
Ribbentrop, Joachim 2 (see also Molotov)
right-wing 26, 40, 95, 99, 115
River Plate, Battle of 29
rivers 158-60, 165
  crossings 158-60, 162, 163, 165-6
  Meuse 23
  Plate 29
  Rhine 23, 158, 162, 163, 165-6
  Volga 117
  Waal 165
road 23, 27, 85, 86, 87, 164, 165, 166, 171
rocket 180-1
roll-on/roll-off 124
Roman Republic 19
Romania 32, 34, 56, 57, 102-3
Rome 85, 86
Rommel, General 36, 54, 71, 72
Rooke, Admiral 118
Roosevelt, President 40-43, 46, 97, 98, 100, 123, 128, 169, 170, 171, 172
Roth, Philip 99
Royal Navy (see British navy)
royalists 57
Ruhr 158
Rupert of the Rhine 161
Russia (USSR, Soviet Union)
  America 21, 35, 43, 46-9, 72, 77, 98, 123-4, 181, 185-6, 182, 184-6
  armed forces 1, 21, 32, 59, 78, 84, 115, 174, 183, 185
  Britain 1-2, 6, 21, 31, 32-3, 35, 36, 44-9, 95, 114, 123-4, 182, 185-6
  espionage 124, 174-5, 181
  Finland 17, 30-1, 32, 59
  France 6, 8-9, 20, 21, 31, 33, 113-8,

123
Germany 1, 2, 5, 13, 18, 19, 32-3, 36, 44, 45, 47, 55, 59-60, 65, 113-20, 132-3, 169, 174-5, 179, 181
  ideology 1, 2, 5, 11, 45-6, 49-50, 57-8, 63, 65, 95, 113, 115, 175-6
Iran 44-9
Japan 17, 19, 47, 149-51, 173, 175, 182-6
Poland 9, 17, 47, 119, 175
post-war 35, 43, 47, 50, 53, 84, 98, 99, 118, 123-4, 175, 181,186
prisoners 59, 60, 130, 132-3
Revolution 59, 64-5
Spain 5-6, 35
tanks 62, 63, 64-5, 68, 72, 78

7th Armoured Division 73, 75
SAS 77, 128
SAVAK 49
SBS 128
SOE 127
SS 78, 103-4, 165
STASI 49
sack(ing) 93, 94, 154, 163, 168
sailor 70, 80, 135, 141, 152, 172-3
St Lucia 41
St Petersburg 116, 117, 119
Saint-Cyr 152
Sakhalin 186
salient 159, 164
Samuel, Herbert 96
Sanders, Bernie 99, 100
Sandhurst College 152, 156
Sandhurst School 156
Scandinavia 33, 38
Scapa Flow 137
Scharnhorst 135, 147, 148
Scheldt 161-2
Schlieffen Plan 24, 27
schnorkel 153-4
Schweinfurt 90
Schwerpunkt 165
sea (see also ocean) 1, 44, 56, 68, 116, 139, 146, 150, 161, 184
  Baltic 31, 59, 117, 119
  Coral 80
  Mediterranean (see main entry)
  North 30, 31
Second Gulf War 113
Second World War
  aces of 77-8
  airmindness 84
  best soldiers 164, 167

boffins 152
bombing 89
causes of 4, 8, 19
combatants 16
ethnic cleansing 101, 104, 105, 110
Grand Strategy 30
invasions during 38-9
material 21, 78
naval 135, 137, 144, 147
neutrality 35
outcome 33, 34, 119, 182, 186
perceptions of 3, 4, 59
presidents 40, 100, 169
tank war 61
unadvised theatres 56
west vs east 21
Second World War 95
secret
  agents 124, 125-6
  atom 124
  intelligence 175
  outstations 78
  police 49-50
  services 125-6
Secretary (see minister)
self-determination 10
self-propelled gun 61-2, 78
Semitic
  anti- 94, 96-7, 102
  pro- 94
Senate 42
Senior Service 137 (see British navy)
separatists 45, 106
Serbia 57, 107-109
service 127, 130, 143
  armed (see main entry)
  chief 167
  secret 125-6
Shah of Iran 45, 46, 49
Shankly, Bill 19
Sherman (tank) 69-70
Shinwell, Emanuel 95
shipbuilding 91, 139, 143, 149
shipping
  convoy (see main entry)
  German 29-33
  iron ore 31
  liner 135
  losses 78, 137, 139
  supply 29, 41, 124, 161
  tankers 48, 144
ships (naval)
  battle- (see main entry)
  battlecruiser 147-8
  CAM 144
  corvette 139, 140

cruiser 29, 138, 148
destroyer 32, 41, 138, 169
submarine (see main entry)
see also individual ship
  Altmark 29-33
  Bismarck 148
  Courageous 144
  Dreadnought 147, 149
  Glorious 149
  Gneisenau 135
  Graf Spee 29, 30, 123
  Hood 148
  Prince of Wales 148
  Queen Elizabeth 82
  Rawalpindi 135-6
  Scharnhorst 135, 147, 149
  Tirpitz 148
  Valiant 82
shooting 133, 134, 141, 150, 167
shortage 33, 68, 132-3, 169
shtetl 104
Sicily 33
Sick Man 8, 12
Sierra Leone 39
Sikh 111
Singapore 149
sinkings 78, 145
skirmish 16, 17
Slovenia 131
slump, economic 40-1, 176-7
sniper 78
snooker 48
socialism 11, 100
society 27, 63, 94, 101-2, 133, 135, 152
soft underbelly 118
soldiers
  American 127, 133, 157, 162
  Australian 85-6
  British 24, 36, 48-9, 72, 84, 94, 127,
    133, 152, 157, 162
  Canadian 161
  Czech 9
  French 24, 86
  German 57, 85, 133, 152
  neutrals 34
  Japanese 130, 135, 136, 172-3
  New Zealand 85
  Russian 59, 60, 62, 130, 132-3, 175
Somalia 39
something must be done 5, 87, 118, 145
sonar (ASDIC) 138
South
  Africa 45, 105, 146
  Asia 45
  Atlantic 29
  -east Asia 173

Pacific 172, 173
Tyrol 4
Soviet Union (see Russia)
Spain 34-36, 40, 118
  Civil War 5, 34
  Inquisition 102
spearhead 23, 74, 165
Special Forces 128
Special Operations Executive 127
specifications 21, 69, 122
Speer, Albert 178
sphere of influence 4, 44
spies 124, 126
sport 77, 121, 131
spring 27-8, 148, 179
Srebrenica 110
Staff 48, 55. 138-9, 152
  German General 22, 23, 60, 152, 179,
       184
Stakhanov, Alexsei 78
Stalin, Joseph
  administrator 167, 173-4
  Churchill 58
  collectivisation 106
  dictator 3, 5
  Hitler 31-2, 33, 116, 118, 120
  Iran 45, 47
  leftist 115
  negotiator 1-2, 43, 58, 182
  tanks 63, 65
  war leader 173-5
Stalingrad 116, 117, 119-20, 133
start line 64, 66, 76, 87
starvation 31, 47, 107, 172
State Department 42, 47
statistics 135, 153-4
stereotype 97, 136
Stilwell, General 128
straits
  Gibraltar 35
  Turkey 36
strategic bombing (see bombing)
strategy 51, 82, 128, 168
  America 42, 85, 128, 158, 164, 169-72
  Britain 32, 42, 44, 53, 72, 74, 85, 90-1,
        128, 141, 158, 164, 167,
        168-9
  France 20
  Germany 18, 22, 33, 54, 85, 119, 158,
        178-9
  Grand 29, 30, 32, 33, 42, 119, 168, 172,
        173, 174, 178
  Japan 173
  Russia 174
submarine (inc U-boats) 48, 138-40, 143
  American 78, 147, 171

anti- 138, 140, 142, 144, 145, 152-3
  bases 41, 54, 138, 143
  British 143, 148
  German 35, 41, 54, 78, 137, 138, 139,
       140, 142, 143, 144, 152-3
  midget 82, 148
Sudan 39
Sudetenland 105
Suez 53, 146
suicide 164, 165, 177
summer 1, 48, 115, 121
superior(ity) 78, 81, 107, 133, 160-1,
       171, 173
  comfortable 21
  overwhelming 21, 85, 173
supply 29, 36, 41, 44, 46-7, 161
  food 35, 47, 168
  minerals 36
  oil 32, 56, 119-20
surface 30, 138, 139, 140
surprise 23, 24, 164, 175
surrender
  Belgium 24, 26
  France 24, 25-28
  Germany 26, 30, 182
  Japan 182-3, 185-6
  sailors 135-6
  troops 72, 119, 125, 130, 133, 161
  unconditional 183, 185
survival 80-81, 133, 135, 139, 166
  of the fittest 176
Sweden 31, 32, 37, 38, 110, 117
Sword of Honour 84
Syria 26, 38, 39, 52, 118
system
  American 42, 77, 169, 170
  British 94, 121, 167-8, 172, 179
  communication 166
  Continental 118
  German 179
  Great Power 8, 52, 59, 113-4, 116-7
  honours 136
  Japanese 172
  Russian 59
  Versailles 8, 12
  weapon 51, 78-9

T-34 46
TASS 186
tactic(al) 72, 74, 81, 95, 162
  aircraft 74, 75, 84, 87, 162
  doctrine 74, 75-6
  military 23, 72, 81, 84, 86, 138
  political 47, 95
Taliban 134

tank (including Panzer) see also
                armoured
  aces 78
  American 46, 63, 65, 69-70, 72, 78, 85,
                141
  anti- 67, 68, 70, 75, 78, 87, 165, 166
  British 61, 62-3, 64, 65, 67, 68, 70-2,
                75, 78, 85, 87, 124, 141,
                165, 166
  buffs 72
  cavalry, as 66-7
  commander 26, 27, 71, 78
  concentrated 64-72
  crews 70
  Czech 10
  en masse 64-72
  French 27, 61, 65, 67
  German 23, 27 , 60, 61-2, 63, 65, 68,
                70-2, 74-5, 78, 164-5, 166
  Israeli 65
  names 61-3
  penny packet 64-72
  Russian 46, 62, 63, 65, 69, 72, 78
  terror 62
  theorists 64, 67
  transport 68-9
  -war 61, 63
    see also individual tanks
      KV-1 63
      T-34 46, 63
      Cavalier 62
      Centaur 62
      Challenger II 62-3
      Char B 61, 62, 67
      Churchill 62
      Comet 62
      Cromwell 62
      Cruiser 62
      Crusader 62
      Elephant 62
      Firefly 63
      Grant 63, 67
      Joseph Stalin 63
      Lee 63
      Lion 62
      Mark I, II. III, IV 62
      Matilda 62, 75
      Mouse 62
      Panther 62, 70
      Rat 62
      Sherman 63, 69-70
      Stuart 63
      Tiger 62, 74
tanker 48, 144
Taranto 149
tarpaulin 90

task force 81, 151
Tasmania 106
tea 165, 166
technical 123, 148, 177
technically 30, 62, 70, 94, 98, 121
technique 27, 75, 87, 127
technology 78-9, 84, 90, 92, 107, 123,
                141, 155, 180
Tehran 45, 46, 48, 49
  Conference 185
terrain 84, 165-6, 170
territory
  British 18, 146
  Bulgarian 57
  Croatian 107-9
  French 18, 52
  German 9
  Norwegian 30, 38
  Romanian 57
  Russian 175
  Serbian 107-9
  Turkish 36
terrorism 127
Teschen 8-14
theatre 46, 82, 168, 170, 172
thermonuclear (also see atomic) 154
Thermopylae 56
Third Reich 177
Third Republic 25
Third World War 63, 78-9
Tiger (tank) 62, 74
Tiger Terror 62
Tilsit 116
Tirpitz 148
Tito, Marshall 58
Todt, Fritz 177
Tokyo 107, 182
Tonypandy 95
torpedo 78, 80, 81, 138, 148
  boats 138
tracks (tank) 61, 62, 69
tractors 61
trade 117, 176-7
tradition 30, 38, 44, 63, 97, 158
transport
  hub 59
  infrastructure 45
  planes 162
  rail 68-9
Treasury 42, 97
treaty
  Anglo-German 12
  Russo-German 6, 18, 32, 116
  Russo-Iran 47
  Russo-Japan 17
  Versailles 8, 180

210

trench 27, 61
Trinidad 41
troops
  airborne 85, 86, 87, 162-3, 164, 166
  American 3, 44, 46, 48, 62, 85, 87,
        162-3
  Australian 85-6
  British 3, 22, 31, 38, 44, 48, 56, 57, 62,
        74, 85, 87, 127, 162-3,
        164, 166, 169
  colonial 3
  French 3, 22, 31, 87, 114
  German 23, 33, 53, 57, 72, 85-6, 87,
        118, 119-20, 135, 169
  ground 67, 84-7, 162
  New Zealand 85
  Polish 10
  Russian 44, 175
  Spanish 34, 35
Truman, President 43
Trump, President 116
Tsar Alexander 116, 117, 118
Tsarist 17, 115-6
Tsushima 150, 151
Tudeh 45-6, 49, 50
Tunis 72, 119
Tunisia 33, 39, 52, 72
Turkey 34-6, 111, 115, 118, 120
Tutsis 110
Twin Towers 170
Two-Navy Rule 146
Type VII 139, 140

U-29 144
U-boat (see submarine)
UN (see United Nations)
USA (see America)
USAAF 170
USSR (see Russia)
Udet, Ernst 177
Ukraine 9, 55, 102, 106, 125
Uncles
  Ho 58
  Joe 46
  Sam 46, 58
unconditional surrender 183, 185
underwater 138, 139
unit 23-4, 30, 61-2, 68, 71, 75-6, 78,
      82-3, 104, 108, 109, 128,
      148, 151, 155, 158, 159,
      165, 180
United Nations 39, 134
university 125
Uruguay 39

V2 180
VLR 145
Valiant HMS 82
venereal disease 72
Venezuela 39
vermin 106
Versailles 4
  Conference 43
  inspectors 65
  System 8, 12
  Treaty 8, 180
Vichy 38, 52
Vickers 122
victim 4, 185
Vietminh 58
Vietnam 58, 113
Vigo 35
Villers-Bocage 74, 75, 76
Vlasov Army 132
Volga 117

WASP 69, 97
Waal 165
Waffen SS 78, 164
Wallace, Vice-President 100
Wallis, Barnes 121-2
Wannsee Conference 120
war
  aim 117, 168
  amateurs 121-2, 125-8
  American Civil 19, 40, 63
  annals 72
  Anglo-Dutch 146, 147
  anti-Semitic 96-7
  Bore- 93
  cabinet 153, 182
  civil 6
  Cold 99
  communists 175-6
  conscription 127
  crime 106, 131-2
  Crimean 118
  decision to fight 15-16, 19
  delivery system 78
  dispute resolution 80
  economy 126-7, 178
  Falklands 150
  First World (see main entry)
  fog of 152, 153
  form guide 15-19
  Franco-Prussian 23
  -gaming 22-3
  General Staff 152
  global 128, 154

Great (see First World War)
Great Patriotic 19
Great Power 15-16, 18, 113
Gulf, both 113
Indo-Pakistan 111
industries 92
infrequent 15
Intelligence 125
interesting 95
Jewish ministers 96-7
Korean 77, 113, 123
land/sea 116
last 22, 23
losing 15
leader (military) 155, 167, 184
leader (political) 167-8
ministers 48, 94, 96, 126, 141, 168
modern 26, 36, 77
most documented 184
naval 138, 141, 146, 147
nuclear 19, 154
neutrals in 31, 34-7
open ended 13
Pacific (see main entry)
Peter Principle in 154-5
Phoney 93
-planning 42
precepts of 60
precipitating 175
predicting outcome 15
presidents (US) 169
prevention 9
prisoners of (see POW)
private 169-70
Revolutionary (US) 40
rule of 89
rules of 130, 132
Russo-Finnish 32
Second World (see main entry)
short 18
small 17, 64
Spanish (US) 40
Spanish Civil 5-6, 34
supplies 44, 168
tank 61, 65
thermonuclear 154
Third World 63, 74, 78
total 131, 167
usages of 132
war-war 63
weapons of 180-1
winning 6, 15, 72, 175, 182, 185
Wark, Kirsty 99
Washington D.C. 41-2
Washington, President 40
Watson-Watt, Robert 122

Waugh, Evelyn 84-5
weapon
  atomic 186
  cost efficient 180-1
  kamikaze 81
  long range 180
  most important 63
  most vile 184
  novel 122, 182, 186
  nuclear 19, 51
  package 180
  small arms 82
  super 89
  system 78
weaponry 36, 67, 75
Wehrmacht (see also German army) 13,
          14, 24, 60, 68, 175
Weimar 8, 65, 96
Wellington (bomber) 122
Weltanschauung 115
west(ern)
  Africa 38
  Desert 36, 71, 74, 75
  Europe 54
  Front 2, 30
  Germany 97
  Norway 30
  Powers 174
West, the 17, 21, 54, 102, 114, 135, 157
Weygand, General 26
White House 42, 100, 169
Whitehall 126, 141
Whittle, Frank 123
who, whom? 113
Wilson, President 8, 35, 43
Wingate, General 128
winter 38, 115
wire, the 130
wireless (radio) 25, 27, 46, 137
withdrawal 10, 27, 53, 54, 75-6, 86, 166,
          179, 184
Wittman, Captain 70, 74-6, 79
wolf packs 139
wood 89, 92
Wooden Wonder 92
world
  attention 186
  attitude to Chechens 104
  -beaters 137
  best air forces 84, 89
  best infrastructure 164
  bogeymen 115
  brave new 180
  champions, inventiveness 122
  -class arms industry 9
  communist 58

conquers 63
finest port 161
first ballistic missile 180
foremost military powers 31
free 58
from Pope downwards 86
geopolitics 48
goes to hell 41
happiness in 101
history 19
holocausts 110
hypocrisy 101
judges by association 49
largest armies 173
largest forces 1
largest moving object 147
largest navies 173, 184
least militarily amenable 56
most powerful man 40
old 89
oldest railway 69
only person 34
opinion 47-8
Policeman 8
post-war settlement 43
real importance in 10
record for plane destruction 77
sails round 149-50
secret services 125, 175
sensible to have war 7
Shopkeeper 8
stage 49
strongest army 19
supremacy 51, 137, 176
technical development 178, 180
War 1, 2, 3 (see under First, Second,
            Third etc)
we live in 112
-wide media storm 29

XXX Corps 162, 163, 164, 165

Yalta 47, 182, 185
Yellow Peril 115
Yemen 39
Yugoslavia
  armed forces 57, 127
  Croat/Serb 107, 108
  invaded 33, 38, 39, 57-8
  mass killings 57, 110

Zaire 39
Zero (airplane) 150

Zionists 120
Zyklon-B 107

213

Lightning Source UK Ltd.
Milton Keynes UK
UKHW02f1835090818
327015UK00010B/439/P